THE WORDS OF

Jesus

Reflections for Every Day

William Wray

**CHARTWELL
BOOKS, INC.**

This edition printed in 2007 by
CHARTWELL BOOKS, INC.
A Division of **BOOK SALES, INC.**
114 Northfield Avenue
Edison, New Jersey 08837

ISBN-13: 978-0-7858-2163-2
ISBN-10: 0-7858-2163-5

Printed in Malaysia

CONTENTS

Introduction... 6

DAILY REFLECTIONS

January 19

February 53

March 85

April 119

May 151

June 185

July.. 217

August 251

September 285

October 317

November 351

December 383

Sources *416*

INTRODUCTION

*Everyone who drinks of this water will be thirsty
again, but those who drink of the water that I will
give them will never be thirsty.*

Gospel of St John 4:13–14

Life of Jesus

Most, if not all, of the readers of this introduction will, of course, be
very familiar with the main events of the life of Jesus. However, a
book such as this is perhaps incomplete unless this well-known
territory is once again traversed.

For many Christians, then, the story of Jesus begins when the
angel Gabriel is sent by God to Mary, who is 'espoused to a man
whose name was Joseph' (*Luke* 1:27). She is told that 'thou shalt. . .
bring forth a son, and shalt call his name JESUS' (*Luke* 1:31). Mary
is confused, because she is still a virgin, but Gabriel tells her that
'The Holy Ghost shall come upon thee' (*Luke* 1:35).

The Birth of Christ

The infant Jesus was born in a manger in Bethlehem, because there
was no room at the inn. A group of shepherds heard the news first,
for the angel of the Lord told them that 'a Saviour, which is Christ
the Lord' (*Luke* 2:11) had been born. Then three wise men followed
Jesus' star from the east until it stood over the stable where he lay,
where they 'fell down, and worshipped him' (*Matthew* 2:11). Jesus'
divinity was apparent to others as well. When Mary and Joseph first

took Jesus to the temple, Simeon took him up in his arms and said to God, 'mine eyes have seen thy salvation' (*Luke* 2:30).

But Jesus also had enemies, even then. An angel commanded Joseph to 'flee into Egypt. . .for Herod will seek the young child to destroy him' (*Matthew* 2:13). Herod's death allowed the Holy Family to return to Israel and they made their home in Nazareth.

Even as a child, Jesus displayed special powers that set him apart from others. One day he 'made of that clay twelve sparrows' and 'at the word they took flight' (Gospel of Thomas). Jesus' destiny as a healer also became apparent: 'a certain young man was cleaving wood. . .and the axe fell and cut in sunder the sole of his foot. . . when. . .the young child Jesus. . .ran thither. . .took hold upon the foot. . .and straightway it was healed' (Gospel of Thomas).

When Jesus was twelve years old, the family visited Jerusalem. They left thinking that Jesus was with them, but he had stayed behind in the temple, where all 'were astonished at his understanding'. It was three days before Mary and Joseph found him, when he said to them, 'How is it that ye sought me? Wist ye not that I must be about my Father's business?' (*Luke* 2:47, 49). As a child, then, Jesus was always aware of his destiny: 'I always was and am a perfect man' (Gospel of Pseudo-Matthew 18).

After Jesus had 'increased in wisdom and stature' (*Luke* 2:52), he journeyed from Galilee to Jordan to be baptized by John the Baptist, after which 'the Holy Ghost descended. . .like a dove upon him, and a voice. . .said, Thou art my beloved Son; in thee I am well pleased' (*Luke* 3:22).

The Temptation of Christ

Jesus was then led into the wilderness by God. After he had fasted for forty days and forty nights, the devil tempted him, saying, 'command this stone that it be made bread'. Jesus answered, 'man shall not live by bread alone, but by every word of God' (*Luke* 4:3,

4). Then the devil showed him all the kingdoms of the world and said, 'All this. . .will I give thee. . .If thou. . .wilt worship me' (*Luke* 4:6, 7). Jesus answered, 'Get thee behind me, Satan. . .it is written, Thou shalt worship the Lord thy God' (*Luke* 4:8). Finally, the tempter took him to the pinnacle of the temple. 'If thou be the Son of God, cast thyself down'. Jesus replied, 'Thou shalt not tempt the Lord thy God' (*Matthew* 4:6, 7). At this the devil left Jesus alone.

From that time on, Jesus began to preach. Leaving Nazareth, he journeyed to Capernaum, where he preached and taught. There, all were 'amazed' by his healing and 'the fame of him went out' (*Luke* 4:36, 37). His mission, though, was to 'preach the kingdom of God' (*Luke* 4:43). By word and deed, his aim was to teach people how to live, so that they could enter this kingdom, which was open to all, including sinners. Following the rules was not enough, however: people needed to look into their hearts as well.

But the supreme sacrifice of the Crucifixion was necessary if the people of the world were to be truly saved. All this had apparently been revealed to Jesus, because he foretold that 'the Son of Man is betrayed to be crucified' (*Matthew* 26:2). Jesus had certainly become a problem for the authorities. He had ridden into Jerusalem while his followers cried, 'Hosanna; Blessed is he that cometh in the name of the Lord' (*Mark* 11:9). Then there was the episode in the temple: he 'poured out the changers' money, and overthrew the tables' (*John* 2:15). No doubt about it, they thought, he had to be dealt with.

Jesus' Betrayal and Death

Jesus was to be arrested after the Feast of the Passover. He shared this feast with his disciples, knowing it would be the last time he did so. 'Jesus took bread. . .and said, Take, eat; this is my body' and then 'he took the cup. . .saying. . .this is my blood' (*Matthew* 26:26, 27, 28). It was then that Jesus singled out Judas, his betrayer, by saying to him, 'That thou doest, do quickly' (*John* 13:27). He also told Peter that 'thou shalt thrice deny that thou knowest me' (*Luke* 22:34).

Before his arrest, Jesus was together with his disciples in the Garden of Gethsemane. It was here that Judas 'came to Jesus, and. . . kissed him', after which the authorities 'laid hands on Jesus, and took him' (*Matthew* 26:49, 50). When Peter was asked three times if he was one of Jesus' disciples, he said, 'I know not the man'. As the cock crowed, Peter then recalled Jesus' prophecy, and 'wept bitterly' (*Matthew* 26:74, 75).

Jesus was first taken to the house of Caiaphas, the high priest. 'Art thou then the Son of God?' he was asked. 'Ye say that I am', he replied (*Luke* 22:70). He was then taken before Pontius Pilate, who asked him, 'Art thou the King of the Jews?' Jesus answered, 'Thou sayest it' (*Luke* 23:3). But Pilate 'found no fault in this man' (*Luke* 23:14). At the Feast of the Passover it was the custom to release a prisoner, but when Pontius Pilate asked the crowd whom they preferred they chose Barabbas. They condemned Jesus, saying, 'Let him be crucified' (*Matthew* 27:22).

Pontius Pilate then gave Jesus over to the soldiers: 'And they. . .put on him a scarlet robe. . .platted a crown of thorns. . .put it upon his head. . .and mocked him' (*Matthew* 27:28, 29). Jesus was forced to carry his cross to a place called Golgotha, where 'they crucified him, and two other with him, on either side one, and Jesus in the midst' (*John* 19:18). When Jesus was upon the cross he was mocked by passers-by, who said, 'If thou be the Son of God, come down from the cross' (*Matthew* 27:40). Finally, Jesus 'cried with a loud voice, and gave up the ghost' (*Mark* 15:37). As he did so 'the earth did quake, and the rocks rent' (*Matthew* 27:51) and a nearby centurion exclaimed, 'Truly this man was the Son of God' (*Mark* 15:39).

When evening came, Joseph of Arimathea, one of Jesus' disciples, begged Pilate for the body of Jesus. He then 'laid it in his own new tomb. . .and rolled a great stone to the door' (*Matthew* 27:60).

The Resurrection and the Life

On the morning of the following day, the women who had followed Jesus from Galilee went to the tomb, but 'they found the stone rolled away. . .and found not the body of the Lord Jesus' (*Luke* 24:2, 3). An angel told them that 'he is risen from the dead' (*Matthew* 28:7). Then two of the disciples went to Emmaus, where Jesus came to them. At first, they did not recognize him, but then 'their eyes were opened, and they knew him' (*Luke* 24:31). When they returned to the other disciples, he appeared again, but they were all 'terrified and affrighted' (*Luke* 24:37). Jesus reassured them by saying, 'handle me, and see; for a spirit hath not flesh and bones' (*Luke* 24:39).

Jesus' final message to his disciples was to 'Go ye therefore, and teach all nations' (*Matthew* 28:19). Then 'he was parted from them, and carried up into heaven' (*Luke* 24:51), where he was joyfully received and 'sat on the right hand of God' (*Mark* 16:19).

Ministry of Jesus

The ministry of Jesus was brief by any standards – it lasted perhaps only three years (fewer according to some) – but what he said and did in that time became the foundation of a faith that has reached deeply into the hearts and lives of countless millions of people. Even in a world in which religious observance could be said to be in decline, the presence of Jesus has dimmed but little. Time is still measured in terms of before Christ (BC) and after Christ (AD) (although BCE and CE are now often used). It is nearly two millennia since Jesus said, 'Heaven and earth shall pass away: but my words shall not pass away' (*Mark* 13:31), but his prophecy is as true now as when he uttered it.

Unlike Muhammad, who reputedly dictated the Qu'ran word for word as a guide for the faithful, Jesus did not create a formal religion. Instead, the purpose of his ministry was to 'preach the kingdom of God' (*Luke* 4:43) and show people how to live before he gave his life on the Cross as payment for the sins of the world. It seems he thought that the kingdom of God was not too far away, because he preached, like John the Baptist, 'Repent: for the kingdom of heaven is at hand' (*Matthew* 4:17), and warned that 'the hour is coming' (*John* 5:25). He was assisted in his ministry by a small group of followers, the Twelve Apostles, and a number of other people who were described as his disciples.

Judaic Roots of Jesus' Teaching

Because of the time and place in which he was born, the teaching of Jesus was very much rooted in Judaism, an advanced religion in a world in which paganism was rife. Judaism was an ideal springboard for Christianity in that it was underpinned by a strong belief in God the Father, the giving of alms and the need to lead a virtuous life. So much was Jesus a Jew that some scholars have said that his main aim was to make his fellow Jews look deeply into the Torah (body of traditional Jewish teaching). Jesus' insistence on the sanctity of marriage perhaps owes much to that tradition.

Most Christians view the Sermon on the Mount as a commentary on the Ten Commandments; many see it as containing the central tenets of Christian discipleship. However, the mountainside setting of Matthew's description of this event could well be a reference to Moses, who delivered his divinely revealed laws from Mount Sinai. Perhaps the sermon was intended as a new Torah. When Jesus said 'Think not that I am come to destroy the law, or the prophets: I am come not to destroy, but to fulfil' (*Matthew* 5:17), could it have been an expression of his desire to reinterpret Mosaic law?

The Sermon on the Mount

The sources of the Sermon on the Mount are not immediately apparent. Unlike some other parts of the Synoptic Gospels (Gospels of Matthew, Mark and Luke), it appears to owe little to the Gospel of St Mark. Some scholars suggest that the Gnostic Gospel of Thomas (see below) is one of the sources and that Q (a hypothetical collection of sayings on which the writers of the gospels were reputed to depend) was another. Whatever the truth of these assumptions, the Sermon's central message of love, humility and charity was universal and from it also came some of Jesus' most important teachings, such as the Beatitudes and the Lord's Prayer.

It is only natural, then, that we should begin our examination of Jesus' teaching with some aspects of the Sermon on the Mount. There was perhaps nothing totally new in Jesus' statement that 'whatsoever ye would that men should do to you, do ye even so to them' (*Matthew* 7:12). This principle, often called the 'Golden Rule', is found in many religions. And does the exhortation 'whosoever shall smite thee on thy right cheek, turn to him the other also' (*Matthew* 5:39) go any further than simple pacifism? Perhaps not, but Jesus' teaching soon took a revolutionary turn.

For instance, he not only preached forgiveness but as the Son of God he was able to demonstrate it: 'the Son of Man hath power on earth to forgive sins' (*Matthew* 9:6). What was even more disturbing for some was that he said that God's kingdom could be entered by sinners as well as the righteous. John the Baptist had demanded repentance above all, but Jesus accepted sinners even before they had repented. In the parable of the prodigal son, for instance, there is greater rejoicing over the son that 'was lost, and is found' (*Luke* 15:24) than the son who stayed behind: 'thou art ever with me' (*Luke* 15:31). Similarly, when Jesus was asked why he ate and drank with 'publicans and sinners', he answered 'They that are whole need not a physician; but they that are sick' (*Luke* 5:30, 31).

According to Jesus, 'sinners' could take precedence over the 'righteous'. In a parable, he tells of a Pharisee who does all that is required of him, but only for outward show, and a publican (tax-collector) who knows he is a sinner: 'God be merciful to me a sinner' (*Luke* 18:13). The publican is more exalted than the Pharisee in the eyes of God. Jesus was telling people to look into their hearts, for merely observing the outward form of the religious laws was not enough.

The Forgiveness of Sins

As we have seen, Jesus had the power to forgive sins. This sometimes resulted in the person being physically, as well as spiritually, cured: 'and Jesus. . .said unto the sick of the palsy. . .thy sins be forgiven thee' (*Matthew* 9:2). Healing occupied a central position in Jesus' ministry. During his lifetime it was thought that the battle between good and evil was fought by angels and demons. While angels were there to protect and intercede, caring for the welfare of mankind, demons were constantly lurking in the shadows, ready to snare the unwary soul. Many believed that the sick were possessed by devils so it is understandable that a number of so-called healers and miracle workers claimed to be able to cast them out.

It is not surprising, therefore, that much of Jesus' healing was recorded as being the casting out of devils: 'they brought him many that were possessed by devils: and he cast out the spirits with his word' (*Matthew* 8:16). It was a concept that could readily be understood by the people of that time. Within the Gospels, the faithful were often healed by a touch: 'If I may touch but his clothes, I shall be whole' (*Mark* 5:28). Jesus' growing reputation disturbed the Pharisees, though, and they responded by linking him with Satan: 'He casteth out devils through the prince of the devils' (*Matthew* 9:33, 34).

Although Jesus' outlook was apparently conditioned by the Torah, he 'healed on the sabbath day' (*Luke* 13:14) causing much 'indignation', particularly amongst the Pharisees. However, his critics had no answer when he asked them, with impenetrable logic, whether they would rescue an ox or an ass from a pit on the same day. Some Jews, including Jesus, believed there was a universal spiritual law. He obviously thought it was right to go against the Torah and heal on the Sabbath, if the end was justified.

Jesus also offered the hope of surviving death: 'If a man keep my saying, he shall never see death' (*John* 8:51). There are three instances in the Gospels in which the dead are brought back to earthly life. The raising of Lazarus is perhaps the best-known example: 'And he that was dead came forth' (*John* 11:43, 44). The supreme sacrifice of the Crucifixion and the Resurrection that followed perhaps made believers think that the promise of eternal life was just as real.

The Divinity of Christ

As well as healing, Jesus performed other kinds of miracles. For many, these events support the concept of his divinity. Some of them also served to strengthen the faith of his disciples. For instance, when Simon, James and John had 'toiled all night, and. . .taken nothing', with Jesus' help 'a great multitude of fishes' were caught (*Luke* 5:5, 6). Then, in what is known as the Transfiguration, Jesus leads Peter, James and John up 'an high mountain' where his 'raiment became shining' and then 'appeared unto them Elias with Moses' (*Mark* 9:2, 3, 4). The power of this type of imagery is evident in the way that many people today can easily recall the details of the Feeding of the Five Thousand, say, or Turning the Water into Wine, even if they know little else of the Gospels.

But not everyone believes in the divinity of Christ. The Jews, for instance, have been awaiting the arrival of the Messiah (one who is anointed by God) since long before the time of Jesus. However, most members of the Jewish faith consider that Jesus has failed to fulfil the Messianic prophecies. On the other hand, although many Muslims believe that Jesus really was the Messiah, they regard him as being no more than a great prophet.

A belief in the divinity of Jesus is, of course, central to the faith of most Christians. There is, therefore, no doubt in the minds of many believers that Jesus is the true Messiah. To them, he is literally the son of God. Perhaps he did not fulfil the Messianic prophecies during his time on earth, but he made it clear that he would do so at his Second Coming. But not all 'Christians' accept the divinity of Jesus. For example, although many Unitarians see themselves as 'Christians' in the sense that they live according to the teachings of Christ, they do not subscribe to the concept of the Trinity (Father, Son and Holy Spirit) and so they regard Jesus as having been unequivocally human.

How do we know about Jesus?

Jesus himself did not ever write a book, but instead his words and deeds have been recorded by others. One of the most famous of these was St Paul. After persecuting the early Christians, Paul, or Saul as he was then, met the spirit of Jesus on the road to Damascus. The experience was enough to propel him into preaching Christianity to the Gentiles at a time when Christianity was very much a Jewish sect. Many believe that Christianity would still have been a branch of Judaism without the work of Paul.

In fact, the earliest known Christian writings are the letters, or epistles, that St Paul sent to the churches he established on his travels around the Mediterranean. In spite of his obvious faith, however, it is considered likely that St Paul never actually met Jesus.

After St Paul, it could be said that most of what we know about Jesus is contained within the Four Gospels. The first three Gospels, those of St Matthew, St Mark and St Luke, are reasonably closely related in that they rely on similar sources. Because they can be studied by synopsis (a summary of events taken from the same point of view) they are known as the Synoptic Gospels. The Fourth

Gospel, which is conventionally attributed to St John, differs significantly from the Synoptic Gospels. For instance, within it Jesus speaks at far greater length.

All of the Gospels are clearly biographical in nature. They are perhaps not historical records as we understand the term, because they depend to a great extent on the author's own position with regard to the events described. We cannot know if the events are real or whether they have been seen through the eyes of faith. There also appears to be a distinct reliance on established writings.

Some scholars suggest that the Synoptic Gospels were greatly influenced by the needs experienced by the communities that were served by their writers. Whether that is true or not, there is evidence that all of the writers relied upon a common source of material, which has become known as Q. The discoveries at Nag Hammadi in Egypt added weight to this belief. In December 1945, a sealed jar was discovered that contained some 52 texts, most of which were essentially Gnostic and Christian. Gnosticism is a religious movement that entertains a belief in the value of intuitive spiritual knowledge.

The Gnostic Gospels

For Christians, the Gnostic Gospels were perhaps the most important part of the find. One of these gospels is the Gospel of Thomas, which is described by the author as 'the secret sayings which the living Jesus spoke'. Some of the sayings from the Gospel of Thomas have been quoted in this book. In addition, other Gnostic sources, such as the Book of Thomas and the Gospel of Mary, are represented.

Hard on the heels of the Nag Hammadi finds came the discovery of the Dead Sea Scrolls. Unearthed between 1947 and 1956, they contained fragments of every book of the Hebrew canon (Old Testament) except for the book of Esther. It is quite possible that they had been left by a Jewish sect called the Essenes. Some scholars think that the writers of the Gospels could have used these writings as a source. Others speculate that John the Baptist and Jesus were either members of the Essene community or had direct dealings with it.

It can be seen, therefore, that the Christian message is spread across a wide range of writings. However, it is not the aim of this book to come to any decision as to the legitimacy or otherwise of one source or another. Instead, the intention is to do nothing more than present the reader with a cross-section of the sayings and stories that have been attributed to Jesus over the years. These sayings and tales have one thing in common: they all provide the reader with a profound insight into human nature. Perhaps what is most striking, in view of the immense diversity of the sources, is that a distinctive single voice appears to come through. If the voice is not that of Jesus, it would need to be that of a very great prophet indeed.

The act of comparing and contrasting the sayings in this book will hopefully shed a considerable light on what Jesus and his teachings came to mean in the years after his death. In addition, the book also provides a rich source of reflection for today's Christians as well as those of other faiths who want to discover more of Jesus' wisdom and universal understanding. Whatever interpretation is placed upon them, the power of his words is undeniable. As St John said, these are the words of 'the true Light, which lighteth every man that cometh into the world' (*John* 1:9).

January

January 1

In the beginning was the Word,
and the Word was with God,
and the Word was God.

The same was in the beginning with
God.

All things were made by him;
and without him was not any thing
made that was made.

In him was life; and the life was
the light of men.

And the light shineth in darkness; and
the darkness comprehended it not.

Gospel of St John 1:1–5

January 2

Jesus went unto the Mount of Olives.

And early in the morning he came
again into the temple, and all the people
came unto him; and he sat down,
and taught them.

Gospel of St John 8:1–2

January 3

Watch out that no one mislead you by saying, 'Look here' or, 'Look there', for the child of humankind is within you. Follow him. Those who seek him will find him.

Gospel of Mary 21

January 4

Jesus answered, Verily, verily, I say unto thee, Except a man be born of water and of the Spirit, he cannot enter into the kingdom of God.

Gospel of St John 3:5

January 5

Judas said, 'Why then in truth do some die and some live?'

The master said, 'Whoever is from truth does not die.'

The Dialogue of the Saviour 58–59
(trans. Roberts–Donaldson)

January 6

When they saw the star, they rejoiced
with exceeding great joy.

And when they were come into the
house, they saw the young child with
Mary his mother, and fell down, and
worshipped him: and when they had
opened their treasures, they presented
unto him gifts; gold, and frankincense,
and myrrh.

Gospel of St Matthew 2:10–11

January 7

For God so loved the world, that he gave
his only begotten Son, that whosoever
believeth in him should not perish, but
have everlasting life.

Gospel of St John 3:16

January 8

The Father loveth the Son, and hath given all things into his hand.

He that believeth on the Son hath everlasting life: and he that believeth not the Son shall not see life; but the wrath of God abideth on him.

Gospel of St John 3:35–36

January 9

And in the midst of the seven candlesticks one like unto the Son of man, clothed with a garment down to the foot, and girt about the paps with a golden girdle.

And when I saw him, I fell at his feet as dead. And he laid his right hand upon me, saying unto me, Fear not; I am the first and the last:

I am he that liveth, and was dead; and, behold, I am alive for evermore, Amen; and have the keys of hell and of death.

Revelation 1:13; 17–18

January 10

Verily I say unto you,
Whosoever shall not receive
the kingdom of God as a little child,
he shall not enter therein.

Gospel of St Mark 10:15

January 11

Do not make the kingdom of heaven a desert within you. Do not be proud because of the light that illumines, but be to yourselves as I myself am to you.

Apocryphon of James 13

January 12

And never be you joyful, save when you
behold your brother with love.

Gospel of Hebrews 7 in
Commentary on Ephesians 3,
Jerome

January 13

Salt is good: but if the salt have lost his saltness, wherewith will ye season it? Have salt in yourselves, and have peace one with another.

Gospel of St Mark 9:50

January 14

One who seeks will not stop until one finds. Having found one will be astonished, and having been astonished, one will reign, and having reigned, one will rest.

Gospel of St Thomas 6B
in *The Apocryphal New Testament*
trans. MR James

January 15

Repent: for the kingdom of heaven
is at hand.

Gospel of St Matthew 4:17

January 16

When Salome enquired about
when the things she asked
should be known, the master said,
'When you have trampled the garments
of shame, when the two become one,
and the male with the female
is neither male nor female.'

Gospel of the Egyptians 3
in *The Apocryphal New Testament*
trans. MR James

January 17

Blessed are the merciful:
for they shall obtain mercy.

Gospel of St Matthew 5:7

January 18

To the fool, good and evil
are one and the same.
For the wise person will be nourished
by truth, and will be like a tree
growing by the stream of water.

Book of Thomas 140

January 19

Do not disdain the Lamb,
for without him it is not possible to see
the door. No one divested will
be able to enter unto the King.

Gospel of Philip

January 20

There is nothing from without a man,
that entering into him can defile him:
but the things which come
out of him, those are they that
defile the man.

Gospel of St Mark 7:15

January 21

I would hear, and I would be heard.
Amen.

I would be thought, being wholly thought.
Amen.

I would be washed, and I would wash.
Amen.

Grace danceth. I would pipe; dance ye all.
Amen.

I would mourn: lament ye all.
Amen.

Acts of John 95
in *The Apocryphal New Testament*
trans. MR James

January 22

One day Jesus was walking
with his followers, and they passed the
carcass of a dog.

His followers said,
'How this dog stinks!'

But Jesus said,
'How white are its teeth.'

al-Ghazali,
The Revival of the Religious Sciences 3.108

January 23

Let your light so shine before men,
that they may see your good works,
and glorify your Father
which is in heaven.

Gospel of St Matthew 5:16

January 24

Take heed of the living one
while you are alive, lest you die
and seek to see him and be
unable to do so.

Gospel of Thomas 59

January 25

I am the light of the world:
he that followeth me shall not
walk in darkness, but shall
have the light of life.

Gospel of St John 8:12

January 26

Hasten to be saved without being urged!
Instead, be eager of your
own accord, and, if possible,
arrive even before me;
for thus the Father will love you.

Apocryphon of James

January 27

The next day John seeth Jesus coming unto him, and saith, Behold the Lamb of God, which taketh away the sin of the world. This is he of whom I said, After me cometh a man which is preferred before me: for he was before me.

Gospel of St John 1:29–30

January 28

I am you and you are I, and wherever you
are, I am there, and in all things
am I sown. And from wherever you wish,
you gather me, and when you gather me,
you gather yourself.

Gospel of Eve,
in Epiphanius, *Panarion* 26.3.1

January 29

I am the door: by me if any man enter in,
he shall be saved, and shall go in and out,
and find pasture.

Gospel of St John 10:9

January 30

He is pure, immeasurable mind. He is an aeon-giving aeon. He is life-giving life. He is a blessedness-giving blessed one. He is knowledge-giving knowledge. He is goodness-giving goodness. He is mercy and redemption-giving mercy. He is grace-giving grace, not because he possesses it, but because he gives the immeasurable, incomprehensible light.

Apocryphon of John

January 31

For one who has not known oneself has not known anything, but who has known oneself already has acquired knowledge about the depth of the universe.

Book of Thomas 138

February

February 1

When you come to know yourselves,
then you will become known,
and you will realize that it is you
who are the sons of the living father.
But if you will not know yourselves,
you dwell in poverty and it is
you who are that poverty.

Gospel of Thomas 3

February 2

I am near you like
the clothes on your body.

Manichaean Psalm Book 239.24
in Meyer, *The Unknown Sayings of Jesus*

February 3

There was a man sent from God,
whose name was John.

The same came for a witness, to bear
witness of the Light, that all men through
him might believe.

He was not that Light,
but was sent to bear witness of that Light.

That was the true Light, which lighteth
every man that cometh into the world.

Gospel of St John 1:6–9

February 4

Blessing on one who exists
before coming into being.
For one who exists has been and will be.

Gospel of Philip

February 5

And he saith unto him,
Verily, verily, I say unto you,
Hereafter ye shall see heaven open,
and the angels of God ascending and
descending upon the Son of man.

Gospel of St John 1:51

February 6

Become earnest about the word! For as to the word, its first part is faith; the second, love; the third, works; for from these comes life. For the word is like a grain of wheat; when someone had sown it, he had faith in it; and when it had sprouted, he loved it, because he had seen many grains in place of one. And when he had worked, he was saved, because he had prepared it for food, (and) again he left (some) to sow. So also can you yourselves receive the kingdom of heaven; unless you receive this through knowledge, you will not be able to find it.

Apocryphon of James

February 7

And it came to pass in those days,
that Jesus came from Nazareth of Galilee,
and was baptized of John in Jordan.

And straightway coming up out of the water,
he saw the heavens opened,
and the Spirit like a dove descending
upon him:

And there came a voice
from heaven, saying,
Thou art my beloved Son,
in whom I am well pleased.

Gospel of St Mark 1:9–11

February 8

I am the gate of life.
One who enters through me
enters into life.

The Clementine Homilies 3.52

February 9

Jesus answered and said unto them,
Though I bear record of myself, yet my
record is true: for I know whence I came,
and whither I go; but ye cannot tell
whence I come, and whither I go.

Gospel of St John 8:14

February 10

If they say to you,
'Where did you come from?',
say to them,
'We came from the light, the place where
the light came into being on its own
accord and established itself and became
manifest through their image.'
If they say to you, 'Is it you?', say,
'We are its children, we are the
elect of the living father.'
If they ask you,
'What is the sign of your father in you?',
say to them,
'It is movement and repose.'

Gospel of Thomas 50

February 11

Take heed that ye do not your alms
before men, to be seen of them:
otherwise ye have no reward of your
Father which is in heaven.

Therefore when thou doest thine alms,
do not sound a trumpet before thee,
as the hypocrites do in the
synagogues and in the streets,
that they may have glory of men.
Verily I say unto you,
They have their reward.

Gospel of St Matthew 6:1–2

February 12

This world is a bridge.
Pass over it, but do not build
your house there.

al-Ghazali,
The Revival of the Religious Sciences 3.182

February 13

And ye shall know the truth,
and the truth shall make you free.

Gospel of St John 8:32

February 14

The woman saith unto him, I know that
Messias cometh, which is called Christ:
when he is come, he will tell us all things.

Jesus saith unto her,
I that speak unto thee am he.

Gospel of St John 4:25–26

February 15

Be ye therefore perfect, even as your Father which is in heaven is perfect.

Gospel of St Matthew 5:48

February 16

He said on that day in the Eucharist:
Oh Thou who have mated the
Perfect Light with the Holy Spirit,
mate also our angels with the images!

Gospel of Philip

February 17

The Saviour said, All nature,
all formations, all creatures exist in and
with one another, and they will be
resolved again into their own roots.

Gospel According to Mary Magdalene 4:22

February 18

Verily, verily, I say unto you,
If a man keep my saying,
he shall never see death.

Gospel of St John 8:51

February 19

Peace I bring to thee, my children,
The Sevenfold Peace
Of the Earthly Mother
And the Heavenly Father.
Peace I bring to thy body,
Guided by the Angel of Power; Peace I bring to thy heart,
Guided by the Angel of Love; Peace I bring to thy mind,
Guided by the Angel of Wisdom. Through the Angels of
Power, Love and Wisdom,
Thou shalt travel the Seven Paths
Of the Infinite Garden,
And thy body, thy heart and thy mind
Shall join in Oneness
In the Sacred Flight to the Heavenly Sea of Peace.

Essene Book of Jesus

February 20

Verily I say unto you, No prophet is
accepted in his own country.

Gospel of St Luke 4:24

February 21

Do not take this life for a lord,
so that it takes you as its slave.

al-Ghazali,
The Revival of the Religious Sciences 3.108

February 22

And Jesus sat over against the treasury,
and beheld how the people cast money
into the treasury:
and many that were rich cast in much.

And there came a certain poor widow, and
she threw in two mites, which
make a farthing.

And he called unto him his disciples, and
saith unto them, Verily I say unto you, That
this poor widow hath cast more in, than all
they which have cast into the treasury:

For all they did cast in of their abundance;
but she of her want did cast in all that she
had, even all her living.

Gospel of St Mark 12:41–44

February 23

And the disciples of John
and of the Pharisees used to fast:
and they come and say unto him,
Why do the disciples of John and of the
Pharisees fast, but thy disciples fast not?

And Jesus said unto them,
Can the children of the bridechamber
fast, while the bridegroom is with them?
As long as they have the bridegroom
with them, they cannot fast.

But the days will come,
when the bridegroom shall be taken
away from them, and then shall
they fast in those days.

Gospel of St Mark 2:18–20

February 24

Foxes have holes, and birds of the air have nests; but the Son of man hath not where to lay his head.

Gospel of St Luke 9:58

February 25

When Salome asked,
'How long will death prevail?'
the master answered,
'As long as you women bear children',
not as if life were bad and creation evil,
but so as to teach the order of nature,
for death always follows birth.

Gospel of the Egyptians 1a
in *The Apocryphal New Testament*
trans. MR James

February 26

Jesus answered,
Verily, verily, I say unto thee,
Except a man be born of water
and of the Spirit, he cannot enter into
the kingdom of God.

That which is born of the flesh is flesh;
and that which is born of the Spirit is
spirit.

Gospel of St John 3:5–6

February 27

Let him who seeks
continue seeking until he finds.
When he finds, he will become troubled.
When he becomes troubled,
he will be astonished,
and he will rule over the All.

Gospel of Thomas 2

February 28

Take heed therefore how ye hear:
for whosoever hath,
to him shall be given;
and whosoever hath not,
from him shall be taken even that
which he seemeth to have.

Gospel of St Luke 8:18

February 29

I would be saved, and I would save.
Amen.

I would be loosed, and I would loose.
Amen.

I would be wounded, and I would wound.
Amen.

I would be born, and I would bear.
Amen.

Acts of John 95
in *The Apocryphal New Testament*
trans. MR James

March

March 1

And this preach ye also
and teach them that believe on me
and preach the kingdom of heaven
of my Father.

Epistle of the Apostles 19

March 2

No man also seweth
a piece of new cloth on an old garment:
else the new piece that filled it up
taketh away from the old,
and the rent is made worse.

Gospel of St Mark 2:21

March 3

Now the parable is this: The seed is the word of God.

Those by the way side are they that hear; then cometh the devil,
and taketh away the word out of their hearts, lest they should
believe and be saved.

They on the rock are they, which, when they hear, receive the word
with joy; and these have no root, which for a while believe, and in
time of temptation fall away.

And that which fell among thorns are they, which, when they have
heard, go forth, and are choked with cares and riches and pleasures
of this life, and bring no fruit to perfection.

But that on the good ground are they, which in an honest and good
heart, having heard the word, keep it,
and bring forth fruit with patience.

Gospel of St Luke 8:5–15

March 4

Fear not because of the destruction of
the body but fear much more the power of
darkness.
Remember all that I have said unto you:
If they have persecuted me they
will persecute you also.
Rejoice I have overcome the world.

Coptic Gospel (fragment)

March 5

Verily I say unto you,
whosoever shall not receive
the kingdom of God as a little child,
he shall not enter therein.

Gospel of St Mark 10:15

March 6

Lo! I come unto you with a sign from your Lord. Lo! I fashion for you out of clay the likeness of a bird, and I breathe into it and it is a bird by Allah's leave.

I heal him who was born blind, and the leper, and I raise the dead, by Allah's leave. And I announce to you what you eat and what you store up in your houses.

Lo! herein verily is a portent for you if you are to be believers.

Qur'an 3: 49-50

March 7

It is also written in your law, that the
testimony of two men is true.

I am one that bear witness of myself,
and the Father that sent me
beareth witness of me.

Gospel of St John 8:17–18

March 8

Love one another and obey one another,
that peace may rule always among you.

Epistle of the Apostles 18

March 9

And John was clothed with camel's hair,
and with a girdle of a skin about his loins;
and he did eat locusts and wild honey;

And preached, saying, There cometh one
mightier than I after me, the latchet of
whose shoes I am not worthy
to stoop down and unloose.

I indeed have baptized you
with water: but he shall baptize you
with the Holy Ghost.

Gospel of St Mark 1:6–8

March 10

Never in the heart of a believer
has the love of this life
and the love of the
Hereafter been gathered,
just as water and fire are not
gathered in one jug.

al-Ghazali,
The Revival of the Religious Sciences

March 11

They that are whole
have no need of the physician,
but they that are sick:
I came not to call the righteous,
but sinners to repentance.

Gospel of St Mark 2:17

March 12

The next day John seeth Jesus coming unto him,
and saith, Behold the Lamb of God,
which taketh away the sin of the world.

This is he of whom I said, After me cometh a man which is
preferred before me: for he was before me.

And I knew him not: but that he should be made manifest to
Israel, therefore am I come baptizing with water.

And John bare record, saying, I saw the Spirit descending
from heaven like a dove, and it abode upon him.

And I knew him not: but he that sent me to baptize with
water, the same said unto me, Upon whom thou shalt see the
Spirit descending, and remaining on him, the same is he
which baptizeth with the Holy Ghost.

And I saw, and bare record that this is the Son of God.

Gospel of St John 1:29–34

March 13

And no man putteth new wine
into old bottles:
else the new wine
doth burst the bottles,
and the wine is spilled,
and the bottles will be marred:
but new wine must be put
into new bottles.

Gospel of St Mark 2:22

March 14

Yea, I tell thee truly,

The paths are seven

Through the Infinite Garden,

And each must be traversed

By the body, the heart and the mind As one,

Lest thou stumble and fall

Into the abyss of emptiness.

For as a bird cannot fly with one wing,

So doth thy Bird of Wisdom

Need two wings of Power and Love

To soar above the abyss

To the Holy Tree of Life.

Essene Book of Jesus

March 15

I saw you. You did not see me nor recognise me. I served you as a garment, and you did not know me.

Gospel According to Mary Magdalene 8:11

March 16

If those who lead you say to you,
'See, the kingdom is in the sky',
then the birds of the sky will precede
you. If they say to you,
'It is in the sea', then the fish
will precede you.
Rather, the kingdom is inside of you,
and it is outside of you.

Gospel of Thomas 3

March 17

Ask me what you will that I should teach you and I will show it to you.

Gospel of Bartholomew 4:3
in *The Apocryphal New Testament*
trans. MR James

March 18

It is easier for a camel to go through the eye of a needle, than for a rich man to enter into the kingdom of God.

Gospel of St Mark 10:25

March 19

Let not your heart be troubled:
ye believe in God, believe also in me.

In my Father's house are many mansions:
if it were not so, I would have told you.
I go to prepare a place for you.

And if I go and prepare a place for you,
I will come again, and receive you
unto myself; that where I am,
there ye may be also.

And whither I go ye know,
and the way ye know.

Gospel of St John 14:1–4

March 20

These are they who ply their looms and
weave nothing.

Quoted by Clement of Alexandria in
Stromata, Vol.1, 8:41

March 21

And, behold, there was a man in Jerusalem, whose name was Simeon; and the same man was just and devout, waiting for the consolation of Israel: and the Holy Ghost was upon him.

And it was revealed unto him by the Holy Ghost, that he should not see death, before he had seen the Lord's Christ.

And he came by the Spirit into the temple: and when the parents brought in the child Jesus, to do for him after the custom of the law,

Then took he him up in his arms, and blessed God, and said, Lord, now lettest thou thy servant depart in peace, according to thy word:

For mine eyes have seen thy salvation, Which thou hast prepared before the face of all people;

A light to lighten the Gentiles, and the glory of thy people Israel.

And Joseph and his mother marvelled at those things which were spoken of him.

Gospel of St Luke 2:25–33

March 22

A certain man planted a vineyard, and set an hedge about it, and
digged a place for the winefat, and built a tower,
and let it out to husbandmen, and went into a far country.

And at the season he sent to the husbandmen a servant, that he
might receive from the husbandmen of the fruit of the vineyard.

And they caught him, and beat him, and sent him away empty.

And again he sent another; and him they killed, and many others;
beating some, and killing some.

Having yet therefore one son, his wellbeloved, he sent him also
last unto them, saying, They will reverence my son.

But those husbandmen said among themselves, This is the heir;
come, let us kill him, and the inheritance shall be ours.

And they took him, and killed him,
and cast him out of the vineyard.

What shall therefore the lord of the vineyard do?
he will come and destroy the husbandmen,
and will give the vineyard unto others.

Gospel of St Mark 12:1–3; 5–9

March 23

Hearken to the word, understand
knowledge, love life,
and no one will persecute you,
nor will anyone oppress you,
other than you yourselves.

Apocryphon of James

March 24

But from the beginning of the creation
God made them male and female.

For this cause shall a man leave his father
and mother, and cleave to his wife;

And they twain shall be one flesh:
so then they are no more twain,
but one flesh.

What therefore God hath joined
together, let not man put asunder.

Gospel of St Mark 10:6–9

March 25

Ye judge after the flesh; I judge no man.

And yet if I judge, my judgment is true:
for I am not alone, but I and the Father
that sent me.

Gospel of St John 8:15–16

March 26

Take ye heed, watch and pray: for ye know
not when the time is.

For the Son of man is as a man
taking a far journey, who left his house,
and gave authority to his servants,
and to every man his work,
and commanded the porter to watch.

Watch ye therefore: for ye know not when
the master of the house cometh,
at even, or at midnight, or at the
cockcrowing, or in the morning:

Lest coming suddenly he find you sleeping.

And what I say unto you I say unto all,
Watch.

Gospel of St Mark 13:33–37

March 27

And the Jews' passover was at hand, and
Jesus went up to Jerusalem,

And found in the temple those that sold
oxen and sheep and doves, and the
changers of money sitting:

And when he had made a scourge of
small cords, he drove them all out of the
temple, and the sheep, and the oxen; and
poured out the changers' money, and
overthrew the tables;

And said unto them that sold doves,
Take these things hence; make not my
Father's house an house of merchandise.

Gospel of St John 2:13–16

March 28

No man, when he hath lighted a candle,
covereth it with a vessel,
or putteth it under a bed;
but setteth it on a candlestick,
that they which enter in
may see the light.

Gospel of St Luke 8:16

March 29

For the Lord said unto me:
If ye make not that which is below
in ye above, and the left hand things
the right then ye shall not enter the
kingdom of God.

Acts of Philip 34

March 30

And (I come) confirming that which was before me of the Torah, and to make lawful some of that which was forbidden unto you. I come unto you with a sign from your Lord, so keep your duty to Allah and obey me.

Lo! Allah is my Lord and your Lord, so worship Him.

That is a straight path.

Qur'an 3: 51

March 31

And if a kingdom be divided against itself, that kingdom cannot stand.

And if a house be divided against itself, that house cannot stand.

Gospel of St Mark 3:24–25

April

April 1

And when they came nigh to Jerusalem,
unto Bethphage and Bethany, at the mount of Olives,
he sendeth forth two of his disciples,

And saith unto them, Go your way into the village over
against you: and as soon as ye be entered into it, ye shall find a
colt tied, whereon never man sat; loose him, and bring him.

And they brought the colt to Jesus, and cast their garments on
him; and he sat upon him.

And many spread their garments in the way: and others cut
down branches off the trees, and strawed them in the way.

And they that went before, and they that followed, cried,
saying, Hosanna; Blessed is he that cometh in the name of the
Lord:

Blessed be the kingdom of our father David, that cometh in
the name of the Lord: Hosanna in the highest.

Gospel of St Mark 11:1–2; 7–10

April 2

Then led they Jesus from Caiaphas unto the
hall of judgment: and it was early; and they themselves
went not into the judgment hall, lest they should be defiled;
but that they might eat the passover.

Pilate then went out unto them, and said,
What accusation bring ye against this man?

They answered and said unto him, If he were not a
malefactor, we would not have delivered him up unto thee.

Then said Pilate unto them, Take ye him,
and judge him according to your law. The Jews therefore said
unto him, It is not lawful for us to put any man to death:

That the saying of Jesus might be fulfilled, which he spake,
signifying what death he should die.

Gospel of St John 18:28–32

April 3

Pilate saith unto him, What is truth? And
when he had said this, he went out again
unto the Jews, and saith unto them, I find
in him no fault at all.

But ye have a custom, that I should release
unto you one at the passover:
will ye therefore that I release unto you the
King of the Jews?

Gospel of St John 18:38–39

April 4

Then Pilate therefore took Jesus,
and scourged him.

And the soldiers platted a crown of
thorns, and put it on his head,
and they put on him a purple robe,

And said, Hail, King of the Jews! and
they smote him with their hands.

Gospel of St John 19:1–3

April 5

And from thenceforth Pilate sought to
release him: but the Jews cried out,
saying, If thou let this man go, thou art
not Caesar's friend: whosoever maketh
himself a king speaketh against Caesar.

When Pilate therefore heard that saying,
he brought Jesus forth, and sat down in
the judgment seat in a place that is called
the Pavement, but in the Hebrew,
Gabbatha.

And it was the preparation of the
passover, and about the sixth hour: and
he saith unto the Jews,
Behold your King!

Gospel of St John 19:12–14

April 6

But they cried out, Away with him,
away with him, crucify him. Pilate saith
unto them, Shall I crucify your King?
The chief priest answered,
We have no king but Caesar.

Then delivered he him therefore unto
them to be crucified. And they took
Jesus, and led him away.

And he bearing his cross went forth into
a place called the place of a skull, which
is called in the Hebrew Golgotha:

Where they crucified him, and two other
with him, on either side one,
and Jesus in the midst.

Gospel of St John 19:15–18

April 7

And Pilate wrote a title, and put it on the cross.
And the writing was,

JESUS OF NAZARETH THE KING OF THE JEWS.

This title then read many of the Jews:
for the place where Jesus was crucified was nigh to the city:
and it was written in Hebrew, and Greek, and Latin.

Gospel of St John 19:19–20

April 8

And there came also Nicodemus,
which at the first came to Jesus by night, and brought a
mixture of myrrh and aloes, about an hundred pound weight.

Then took they the body of Jesus,
and wound it in linen clothes with the spices,
as the manner of the Jews is to bury.

Now in the place where he was crucified there was a garden;
and in the garden a new sepulchre,
wherein was never man yet laid.

There laid they Jesus therefore because of the Jews'
preparation day; for the sepulchre was nigh at hand.

Gospel of St John 19:39–42

April 9

And the angel answered and said unto the women,
Fear not ye: for I know that ye seek Jesus,
which was crucified.

He is not here: for he is risen, as he said.
Come, see the place where the Lord lay.

And go quickly, and tell his disciples that he is risen
from the dead; and, behold, he goeth before you into Galilee;
there shall ye see him: lo, I have told you.

And they departed quickly from the sepulchre with fear and
great joy; and did run to bring his disciples word.

Gospel of St Matthew 28:1–4

April 10

Let the dead bury their dead:
but go thou and preach the
kingdom of God.

Gospel of St Luke 9:60

April 11

But of that day and that hour knoweth
no man, no, not the angels which are in
heaven, neither the Son, but the Father.

Gospel of St Mark 13:32

April 12

O you who demand the world
in order to do righteous with it –
leaving the world is more
righteous for you.

al-Ghazali,
The Revival of the Religious Sciences 3.108

April 13

And he said unto them,
Take heed what ye hear:
with what measure ye mete,
it shall be measured to you:
and unto you that hear
shall more be given.

Gospel of St Mark 4:24

April 14

Now Jesus made of that clay twelve sparrows: and it was the
Sabbath day. And a child ran and told Joseph, saying: Behold
the child playeth about the brook, and hath made sparrows of
the clay, which is not lawful. And he when he heard it went
and said to the child: Wherefore doest thou so and profaneth
the Sabbath? But Jesus answered him not, but looked upon
the sparrows and said: Go ye, take your flight and remember
me your life. And at the word they took flight and went up in
the air. And when Joseph saw it he was astonished.

Gospel of Thomas
(Greek Text B 3:1)

April 15

And he said unto them,
Ye are from beneath;
I am from above:
ye are of this world;
I am not of this world.

Gospel of St John 8:23

April 16

Already the time has come,
brothers, for us to abandon
our labour and stand at rest.
For whoever stands at rest
will rest forever.
And I say to you,
be always above time.

The Dialogue of the Savior,
(trans. Emmel)

April 17

Verily, verily, I say unto you,
He that entereth not by the door into the sheepfold,
but climbeth up some other way, the same is a thief and a robber.

But he that entereth in by the door is the shepherd of the sheep.

To him the porter openeth; and the sheep hear his voice: and he
calleth his own sheep by name, and leadeth them out.

And when he putteth forth his own sheep, he goeth before them,
and the sheep follow him: for they know his voice.

And a stranger will they not follow, but will flee from him: for
they know not the voice of strangers.

Gospel of St John 10:1–5

April 18

Rise up and I will reveal unto you that which is above the heaven and in the heaven, and your rest which is in the kingdom of heaven. For my Father hath given me power to take you up thither, and them also that believe on me.

Epistle of the Apostles 12

April 19

When Jesus had spoken these words,
he went forth with his disciples over the brook Cedron,
where was a garden, into the which he entered,
and his disciples.

Judas also, which betrayed him, knew the place:
for Jesus ofttimes resorted thither with his disciples.

Judas then, having received a band of men and officers
from the chief priests and Pharisees,
cometh thither with lanterns and torches and weapons.

Jesus therefore, knowing all things that should come upon
him, went forth, and said unto them, Whom seek ye?

They answered him, Jesus of Nazareth.
Jesus saith unto them, I am he.
And Judas also, which betrayed him, stood with them.

Gospel of St John 18:1–5

April 20

My bread is hunger,
my banner fear,
my clothes are wool,
and my prayer in winter is at sun rise,
and my lamp is the moon.
My ride is my legs,
my food and fruit whatever
the earth produces.
I spend the night and have nothing,
I awake in the morning
and have nothing,
and there is no one upon earth
more richer than I.

al-Ghazali,
The Revival of the Religious Sciences

April 21

Verily I say unto thee that hypocrisy and backbiting is heavier than all sins.

Gospel of Bartholomew 5:1
in *The Apocryphal New Testament*
trans. MR James

April 22

It is the spirit that quickeneth;
the flesh profiteth nothing:
the words that I speak unto you,
they are spirit, and they are life.

Gospel of St John 6:63

April 23

He is not corporeal nor is he incorporeal. He is neither large nor is he small. There is no way to say, 'What is his quantity?' or, 'What is his quality?' for no one can know him. He is not someone among (other) beings, rather he is far superior. Not that he is (simply) superior, but his essence does not partake in the aeons nor in time. For he who partakes in an aeon was prepared beforehand. Time was not apportioned to him, since he does not receive anything from another, for it would be received on loan. For he who precedes someone does not lack, that he may receive from him. For rather, it is the latter that looks expectantly at him in his light.

Apocryphon of John

April 24

It is written, Man shall not live by bread alone, but by every word that proceedeth out of the mouth of God.

Gospel of St Matthew 4:4

April 25

Then saith the woman of Samaria unto him, How is it that
thou, being a Jew, askest drink of me, which am a woman of
Samaria? for the Jews have no dealings with the Samaritans.

Jesus answered and said unto her, If thou knewest the gift of
God, and who it is that saith to thee, Give me to drink;
thou wouldest have asked of him,
and he would have given thee living water.

The woman saith unto him, Sir, thou hast nothing
to draw with, and the well is deep:
from whence then hast thou that living water?

Art thou greater than our father Jacob, which gave us the well,
and drank thereof himself, and his children, and his cattle?

Jesus answered and said unto her,
Whosoever drinketh of this water shall thirst again:

But whosoever drinketh of the water that I shall give him
shall never thirst; but the water that I shall give him shall be
in him a well of water springing up into everlasting life.

Gospel of St John 4:9–14

April 26

And Jesus said unto him, Go thy way;
thy faith hath made thee whole.

Gospel of St Mark 10:52

April 27

Verily, O master, all things that proceed
out of my mouth are true.
And I am before all men, and I am Lord,
but ye are the children of strangers,
for unto me is given the glory of the
worlds but unto you is nothing given:
for I am before all worlds.

Gospel of Thomas
(Latin Text 6:2)

April 28

The thief cometh not, but for to steal,
and to kill, and to destroy:
I am come that they might have life,
and that they might have it more
abundantly.

Gospel of St John 10:10

April 29

And they came to Jericho: and as he went out of Jericho with
his disciples and a great number of people, blind Bartimaeus,
the son of Timaeus, sat by the highway side begging.

And when he heard that it was Jesus of Nazareth, he began to
cry out, and say, Jesus, thou Son of David, have mercy on me.

And many charged him that he should hold his peace:
but he cried the more a great deal,
Thou Son of David, have mercy on me.

And Jesus stood still, and commanded him to be called.
And they call the blind man, saying unto him,
Be of good comfort, rise; he calleth thee.

And he, casting away his garment, rose, and came to Jesus.

And Jesus answered and said unto him,
What wilt thou that I should do unto thee? The blind man
said unto him, Lord, that I might receive my sight.

And Jesus said unto him, Go thy way; thy faith hath made
thee whole. And immediately he received his sight, and
followed Jesus in the way.

Gospel of St Mark 10:46–52

April 30

So when the Samaritans were come
unto him, they besought him that he
would tarry with them:
and he abode there two days.

And many more believed because of his
own word.

Gospel of St John 4:40–41

May

May 1

Do ye think it a thing incredible that I have told you the truth? I know when ye were born and your fathers; and if I say more unto you I know when the world was created, and who sent me unto you.

Gospel of Thomas
(Latin Text 6:4)

May 2

Then Jesus said unto them, Verily, verily, I say unto you,
Except ye eat the flesh of the Son of man, and drink his blood,
ye have no life in you.

Whoso eateth my flesh, and drinketh my blood,
hath eternal life; and I will raise him up at the last day.

For my flesh is meat indeed, and my blood is drink indeed.

He that eateth my flesh, and drinketh my blood,
dwelleth in me, and I in him.

As the living Father hath sent me, and I live by the Father:
so he that eateth me, even he shall live by me.

Gospel of St John 6:53–57

May 3

Now as he walked by the sea of Galilee,
he saw Simon and Andrew his brother
casting a net into the sea:
for they were fishers.

And Jesus said unto them,
Come ye after me, and I will make you to
become fishers of men.

And straightway they forsook their nets,
and followed him.

Gospel of St Mark 1:16–18

May 4

Think not that I am come to
destroy the law, or the prophets:
I am not come to destroy, but to fulfil.

Gospel of St Matthew 5:17

May 5

Why seek ye me?
Know ye not that I must be
in my Father's house?

Gospel of Thomas,
(Greek Text A 19:1)

May 6

For when they shall rise from the dead,
they neither marry, nor are given in
marriage; but are as the angels
which are in heaven.

And as touching the dead, that they rise:
have ye not read in the book of Moses,
how in the bush God spake unto him,
saying, I am the God of Abraham, and
the God of Isaac, and the God of Jacob?

He is not the God of the dead,
but the God of the living.

Gospel of St Mark 12:25–27

May 7

Then were there brought unto him little children, that he should put his hands on them, and pray: and the disciples rebuked them.

But Jesus said, Suffer little children, and forbid them not, to come unto me: for of such is the kingdom of heaven.

Gospel of St Matthew 19:13–15

May 8

Jesus said unto them, Verily, verily, I say unto you, Before Abraham was, I am.

Gospel of St John 8:58

May 9

I would flee, and I would stay.
Amen.

I would adorn, and I would be adorned.
Amen.

I would be united, and I would unite.
Amen.

Acts of John 95
in *The Apocryphal New Testament*
trans. MR James

May 10

No man, having put his hand to the plough, and looking back, is fit for the kingdom of God.

Gospel of St Luke 9:62

May 11

I have cast fire upon the world, and see,
I am guarding it until it blazes.

Gospel Of Thomas 10

May 12

And immediately the Spirit driveth him
into the wilderness.

And he was there
in the wilderness forty days,
tempted of Satan; and was with
the wild beasts; and the angels
ministered unto him.

Gospel of St Mark 1:12–13

May 13

The nobleman saith unto him, Sir, come down ere my child die.

Jesus saith unto him, Go thy way; thy son liveth.
And the man believed the word that Jesus had
spoken unto him, and he went his way.

And as he was now going down, his servants met him,
and told him, saying, Thy son liveth.

Then inquired he of them the hour when he began to amend.
And they said unto him, Yesterday at the seventh hour
the fever left him.

So the father knew that it was at the same hour,
in the which Jesus said unto him, Thy son liveth: and himself
believed, and his whole house.

This is again the second miracle that Jesus did,
when he was come out of Judaea into Galilee.

Gospel of St John 4:49–54

May 14

And if Satan rise up against himself, and be divided, he cannot stand, but hath an end.

Gospel of St Mark 3:26

May 15

Mary was alarmed for him, but he said,
Fear not, neither conceive that
I am a child, for I always was and am a
perfect man, and it is necessary
that all the beasts of the forest should
grow tame before me.

Gospel of Pseudo-Matthew 18

May 16

The harvest truly is great,
but the labourers are few:
pray ye therefore the Lord of the harvest,
that he would send forth labourers into
his harvest.

Gospel of St Luke 10:2

May 17

And when Jesus came into the ruler's
house, and saw the minstrels and the
people making a noise,

He said unto them, Give place:
for the maid is not dead, but sleepeth.
And they laughed him to scorn.

But when the people were put forth,
he went in, and took her by the hand,
and the maid arose.

Gospel of St Matthew 9:23–25

May 18

And as they did eat, Jesus took bread,
and blessed, and brake it, and gave to
them, and said, Take, eat: this is my body.

And he took the cup, and when he had
given thanks, he gave it to them: and
they all drank of it.

And he said unto them,
This is my blood of the new testament,
which is shed for many.

Verily I say unto you, I will drink no
more of the fruit of the vine,
until that day that I drink it new in the
kingdom of God.

Gospel of St Mark 14:22–25

May 19

And ye yourselves like unto men that wait for their lord, when he will return from the wedding; that when he cometh and knocketh, they may open unto him immediately.

Blessed are those servants, whom the lord when he cometh shall find watching: verily I say unto you, that he shall gird himself, and make them to sit down to meat, and will come forth and serve them.

And if he shall come in the second watch, or come in the third watch, and find them so, blessed are those servants.

Gospel of St Luke 12:36–37

May 20

Let your light so shine before men,
that they may see your good works,
and glorify your Father
which is in heaven.

Gospel of St Matthew 5:16

May 21

O disciples, be satisfied with the
minimum of the world,
with the safety of religion,
as the companions of the
world are satisfied
with the minimum of religion
and the safety of the world.

al-Ghazali,
The Revival of the Religious Sciences 3.108

May 22

Blessed are the pure in heart:
for they shall see God.

Gospel of St Matthew 5:8

May 23

The wisdom which humans call barren is
herself the Mother of the Angels.
And the Companion of the Christ is
Mariam the Magdalene.
The Lord loved Mariam more than all
the other Disciples, and he kissed her
often on her mouth.
The other women saw his love for
Mariam, they say to him:
Why do thou love her more than
all of us? The Saviour replied,
he says to them:
Why do I not love you as I do her?

Gospel of Philip 59

May 24

Therefore doth my Father love me,
because I lay down my life,
that I might take it again.

No man taketh it from me,
but I lay it down of myself.
I have power to lay it down,
and I have power to take it again.
This commandment have I
received of my Father.

Gospel of St John 10:17–18

May 25

Let the unfruitful bear fruit, and the
blind see, and the lame walk straight,
and the poor enjoy good things,
and the dead revive, and everyone
return into a restored state,
and abide in him who is the root of life
and of everlasting sweetness.

Gospel of Pseudo-Matthew 31

May 26

Then came Peter to him, and said, Lord,
how oft shall my brother sin against me,
and I forgive him? till seven times?

Jesus saith unto him, I say not unto thee,
Until seven times: but,
Until seventy times seven.

Gospel of St Matthew 18:21–22

May 27

For there is nothing hid,
which shall not be manifested;
neither was any thing kept secret,
but that it should come abroad.

Gospel of St Mark 4:22

May 28

He is illimitable, since there is no one prior to him
to set limits to him. He is unsearchable,
since there exists no one prior to him to examine him.
He is immeasurable, since there was no one prior
to him to measure him. He is invisible,
since no one saw him. He is eternal,
since he exists eternally. He is ineffable,
since no one was able to comprehend him to
speak about him. He is unnameable,
since there is no one prior to
him to give him a name.

He is immeasurable light,
which is pure, holy (and) immaculate.
He is ineffable, being perfect in incorruptibility.
(He is) not in perfection, nor in blessedness,
nor in divinity, but he is far superior.

Apocryphon of John

May 29

Say not ye, There are yet four months,
and then cometh harvest?
behold, I say unto you, Lift up your eyes,
and look on the fields;
for they are white already to harvest.

And he that reapeth receiveth wages,
and gathereth fruit unto life eternal:
that both he that soweth and he that
reapeth may rejoice together.

Gospel of St John 4:35–36

May 30

For your sakes I have placed myself under
the curse, that you may be saved.

Apocryphon of James 13

May 31

Blessed are the poor in spirit:
for theirs is the kingdom of heaven.

Gospel of St Matthew 5:3

June

June 1

Now it came to pass, as they went, that he entered
into a certain village: and a certain woman named Martha
received him into her house.

And she had a sister called Mary, which also
sat at Jesus' feet, and heard his word.

But Martha was cumbered about much serving, and came to
him, and said, Lord, dost thou not care that my sister hath left
me to serve alone? bid her therefore that she help me.

And Jesus answered and said unto her, Martha, Martha, thou
art careful and troubled about many things:

But one thing is needful: and Mary hath chosen that good
part, which shall not be taken away from her.

Gospel of St Luke 10:38–42

June 2

The Saviour said, 'All nature, all formations, all creatures exist in and with one another, and they will be resolved again into their own roots.'

Gospel According to Mary Magdalene 4:22

June 3

And, behold, a woman in the city,
which was a sinner, when she knew that
Jesus sat at meat in the Pharisee's house,
brought an alabaster box of ointment,

And stood at his feet behind him weeping,
and began to wash his feet with tears,
and did wipe them with the hairs of her
head, and kissed his feet, and anointed
them with the ointment.

Gospel of St Luke 7:37–38

June 4

Blessed are the peacemakers:
for they shall be called the
children of God.

Gospel of St Matthew 5:9

June 5

The light of the body is the eye:
therefore when thine eye is single,
thy whole body also is full of light;
but when thine eye is evil,
thy body also is full of darkness.

Gospel of St Luke 11:34

June 6

I am the good shepherd: the good shepherd giveth his life for the sheep.

But he that is an hireling, and not the shepherd, whose own the sheep are not, seeth the wolf coming, and leaveth the sheep, and fleeth: and the wolf catcheth them, and scattereth the sheep.

The hireling fleeth, because he is an hireling, and careth not for the sheep.

I am the good shepherd, and know my sheep, and am known of mine.

Gospel of St John 10:11–14

June 7

Be not grieved, but let thy heart rejoice and be glad; for thou hast found grace to behold the glory that was given me of my Father Virgin. And the holy mother of God looked up and saw in him glory which the mouth cannot utter nor comprehend.

'Assumption of the Virgin' in
The Apocryphal New Testament

June 8

For verily I say unto you,
Till heaven and earth pass, one jot or one
tittle shall in no wise pass from the law,
till all be fulfilled.

Gospel of St Matthew 5:18

June 9

Now when he came nigh to the gate of the city, behold, there was a dead man carried out, the only son of his mother, and she was a widow: and much people of the city was with her.

And when the Lord saw her, he had compassion on her, and said unto her, Weep not.

And he came and touched the bier: and they that bare him stood still. And he said, Young man, I say unto thee, Arise.

And he that was dead sat up, and began to speak. And he delivered him to his mother.

Gospel of St Luke 7:12–14

June 10

And when Jesus departed thence,
two blind men followed him, crying,
and saying, Thou Son of David,
have mercy on us.

And when he was come into the house,
the blind men came to him:
and Jesus saith unto them,
Believe ye that I am able to do this? They
said unto him, Yea, Lord.

Then touched he their eyes, saying,
According to your faith be it unto you.

And their eyes were opened;
and Jesus straitly charged them, saying,
See that no man know it.

Gospel of St Matthew 9:27–30

June 11

Thou that dancest, perceive what I do, for thine is this passion of the manhood, which I am about to suffer. For thou couldest not at all have understood what thou sufferest if I had not been sent unto thee, as the word of the Father.

Acts of John 96
in *The Apocryphal New Testament*
trans. MR James

June 12

Where the mind is, there is the treasure.

Gospel According to Mary Magdalene 5:9

June 13

When he was come down from the mountain, great multitudes followed him.

And, behold, there came a leper and worshipped him, saying, Lord, if thou wilt, thou canst make me clean.

And Jesus put forth his hand, and touched him, saying, I will; be thou clean. And immediately his leprosy was cleansed.

Gospel of St Matthew 8:1–3

June 14

Now when he had left speaking, he said unto Simon, Launch out into the deep, and let down your nets for a draught.

And Simon answering said unto him, Master, we have toiled all the night, and have taken nothing: nevertheless at thy word I will let down the net.

And when they had this done, they inclosed a great multitude of fishes: and their net brake.

And they beckoned unto their partners, which were in the other ship, that they should come and help them. And they came, and filled both the ships, so that they began to sink.

When Simon Peter saw it, he fell down at Jesus' knees, saying, Depart from me; for I am a sinful man, O Lord.

For he was astonished, and all that were with him, at the draught of the fishes which they had taken.

Gospel of St Luke 5:4–9

June 15

Every soul that calleth upon thy name
shall not be put to shame but shall find
mercy and consolation and succour and
confidence, both in this world and in that
which is to come, before my Father
which is in heaven.

'Assumption of the Virgin' in
The Apocryphal New Testament

June 16

Go your ways: behold,
I send you forth as lambs among wolves.

Gospel of St Luke 10:3

June 17

And a certain man was there, which had an
infirmity thirty and eight years.

When Jesus saw him lie, and knew that he had been now a long
time in that case, he saith unto him, Wilt thou be made whole?

The impotent man answered him, Sir, I have no man, when the
water is troubled, to put me into the pool: but while I am coming,
another steppeth down before me.

Jesus saith unto him, Rise, take up thy bed, and walk.

And immediately the man was made whole, and took up his bed,
and walked: and on the same day was the sabbath.

Gospel of St John 5:5–9

June 18

You are the thinking and the entire serenity of the solitary.

Dialogue of the Savior
(trans. Emmel)

June 19

And after six days Jesus taketh Peter, James, and John his
brother, and bringeth them up into an high mountain apart,

And was transfigured before them: and his face did shine as
the sun, and his raiment was white as the light.

And, behold, there appeared unto them Moses and Elias
talking with him.

Then answered Peter, and said unto Jesus, Lord, it is good for
us to be here: if thou wilt, let us make here three tabernacles;
one for thee, and one for Moses, and one for Elias.

While he yet spake, behold, a bright cloud overshadowed
them: and behold a voice out of the cloud, which said, This is
my beloved Son, in whom I am well pleased; hear ye him.

Gospel of St Matthew 17:1–5

June 20

We are 'children of Light' having been illuminated by 'the dayspring' of the spirit of the Lord 'from on high'.

Secret Gospel According to Mark

June 21

Therefore whatsoever ye have spoken in darkness shall be heard in the light; and that which ye have spoken in the ear in closets shall be proclaimed upon the housetops.

Gospel of St Luke 12:3

June 22

Then the band and the captain and
officers of the Jews took Jesus,
and bound him,

And led him away to Annas first;
for he was father in law to Caiaphas,
which was the high priest that same year.

Now Caiaphas was he,
which gave counsel to the Jews,
that it was expedient that one man
should die for the people.

Gospel of St John 18:12–14

June 23

Ye are the light of the world.
A city that is set on an hill cannot be hid.

Gospel of St Matthew 5:14

June 24

And this is the record of John, when the Jews sent priests and
Levites from Jerusalem to ask him, Who art thou?

And he confessed, and denied not; but confessed,
I am not the Christ.

And they asked him, What then? Art thou Elias? And he
saith, I am not. Art thou that prophet? And he answered, No.

Then said they unto him, Who art thou? that we may give an
answer to them that sent us. What sayest thou of thyself?

He said, I am the voice of one crying in the wilderness, Make
straight the way of the Lord, as said the prophet Esaias.

Gospel of St John 1:19–23

June 25

Jesus went unto the mount of Olives.

And early in the morning he came again into the temple,
and all the people came unto him; and he sat down,
and taught them.

And the scribes and Pharisees brought unto him
a woman taken in adultery; and when they had set
her in the midst,

They say unto him, Master, this woman
was taken in adultery, in the very act.

Now Moses in the law commanded us,
that such should be stoned: but what sayest thou?

This they said, tempting him, that they might have to accuse
him. But Jesus stooped down, and with his finger wrote on
the ground, as though he heard them not.

So when they continued asking him, he lifted up himself,
and said unto them, He that is without sin among you,
let him first cast a stone at her.

Gospel of St John 8:1–7

June 26

Blessed are they which do hunger
and thirst after righteousness:
for they shall be filled.

Gospel of St Matthew 5:6

June 27

Verily you preach and proclaim as I
command you, for I will be with you, for
it is my good pleasure to be with you,
that you may be heirs with me in
the kingdom of heaven, even the
kingdom of him that sent me.

Epistle of the Apostles 19

June 28

Marvel not that I said unto thee,
Ye must be born again.

The wind bloweth where it listeth,
and thou hearest the sound thereof,
but canst not tell whence it cometh,
and whither it goeth:
so is every one that is born of the Spirit.

Gospel of St John 3:7–8

June 29

And when they were gone over, they came into the land of Gennesaret.

And when the men of that place had knowledge of him, they sent out into all that country round about, and brought unto him all that were diseased;

And besought him that they might only touch the hem of his garment: and as many as touched were made perfectly whole.

Gospel of St Matthew 14:34–36

June 30

Let your loins be girded about,
and your lights burning.

Gospel of St Luke 12:35

July

July 1

He does not see through the soul nor through the spirit, but the mind which [is] between the two – that is [what] sees the vision…

Gospel According to Mary Magdalene 5:11

July 2

Blessed are they which are persecuted for righteousness' sake: for theirs is the kingdom of heaven.

Gospel of St Matthew 5:10

July 3

And after these things he went forth, and saw a publican,
named Levi, sitting at the receipt of custom:
and he said unto him, Follow me.

And he left all, rose up, and followed him.

And Levi made him a great feast in his own house:
and there was a great company of publicans and of others
that sat down with them.

But their scribes and Pharisees murmured against his disciples,
saying, Why do ye eat and drink with publicans and sinners?

And Jesus answering said unto them,
They that are whole need not a physician; but they that are sick.

I came not to call the righteous, but sinners to repentance.

Gospel of St Luke 5:27–32

July 4

For God sent not his Son
into the world to condemn the world;
but that the world through him
might be saved.

Gospel of St John 3:17

July 5

Verily I say unto you
ye shall be my brethren and my friends,
for my Father hath found pleasure in you:
and so shall they be that believe
on me by your means.

Epistle of the Apostles 19

July 6

Sister, no one will be able to
inquire about these things except for
someone who has somewhere to
put them in his heart.

Dialogue of the Savior
(trans. Emmel)

July 7

And I say unto you my friends,
Be not afraid of them that kill the body,
and after that have no more
that they can do.

Gospel of St Luke 12:4

July 8

Where the Spirit of the Lord
is there is liberty.

Secret Gospel According to Mark

July 9

Blessed are ye, when men shall revile you,
and persecute you, and shall say all manner
of evil against you falsely,
for my sake.

Rejoice, and be exceeding glad:
for great is your reward in heaven:
for so persecuted they the prophets
which were before you.

Gospel of St Matthew 5:11–12

July 10

As they went out, behold,
they brought to him a dumb man
possessed with a devil.

And when the devil was cast out,
the dumb spake: and the
multitudes marvelled, saying,
It was never so seen in Israel.

But the Pharisees said, He casteth out
devils through the prince of the devils.

Gospel of St Matthew 9:32–34

July 11

Matthew said:
'How does the small join
itself to the big?'

The Lord said,
'When you abandon the works
which will not follow you,
then you will rest.'

Dialogue of the Savior
(trans. Emmel)

July 12

But rather seek ye the kingdom of God;
and all these things shall be
added unto you.

Gospel of St Luke 12:31

July 13

This heaven will pass away,
and the one above it will pass away.
The dead are not alive, and the living will
not die. In the days when you consumed
what is dead, you made it what is alive.
When you come to dwell in the light,
what will you do? On the day when you
were one you became two.
But when you become two,
what will you do?

Gospel Of Thomas 11

July 14

And Peter answered him and said, Lord, if it be thou,
bid me come unto thee on the water.

And he said, Come. And when Peter was come down out of the
ship, he walked on the water, to go to Jesus.

But when he saw the wind boisterous, he was afraid;
and beginning to sink, he cried, saying, Lord, save me.

And immediately Jesus stretched forth his hand,
and caught him, and said unto him, O thou of little faith,
wherefore didst thou doubt?

And when they were come into the ship, the wind ceased.

Then they that were in the ship came and worshipped him,
saying, Of a truth thou art the Son of God.

Gospel of St Matthew 14:28–33

July 15

The heavens and the earth
will be rolled up in your presence.
And the one who lives from the living
one will not see death.

Gospel Of Thomas 111

July 16

I am wholly in the Father and the Father in me, because of the likeness of the form and the power and the fullness and the light and the measure and the voice.

Epistle of the Apostles 17

July 17

And when he had gone a little further
thence, he saw James the son of Zebedee,
and John his brother, who also were in
the ship mending their nets.

And straightway he called them:
and they left their father Zebedee in
the ship with the hired servants,
and went after him.

Gospel of St Mark 1:19–20

July 18

That which supports the earth is that
which supports the heaven.
When a Word comes forth from the
Greatness, it will come on what supports
the heaven and the earth.
For the earth does not move.
Were it to move, it would fall.
But it neither moves nor falls, in order
that the First Word might not fail.
For it was that which established the
cosmos and inhabited it,
and inhaled fragrance from it.

Dialogue of the Savior
(trans. Emmel)

July 19

If therefore ye have not been faithful in
the unrighteous mammon, who will commit
to your trust the true riches?

And if ye have not been faithful in that
which is another man's, who shall give you
that which is your own?

Gospel of St Luke 16:11–12

July 20

I have recognised that the All
is being dissolved, both the earthly
(things) and the heavenly.

Gospel According to Mary Magdalene 8:17

July 21

But Simon's wife's mother
lay sick of a fever, and anon
they tell him of her.

And he came and took
her by the hand, and lifted her up;
and immediately the fever left her,
and she ministered unto them.

Gospel of St Mark 1:30–31

July 22

All things are pure to the pure.

Secret Gospel According to Mark

July 23

For the nature of matter is resolved into
the roots of its own nature alone.

Gospel According to Mary Magdalene 4:23

July 24

And when he had sent the multitudes away,
he went up into a mountain apart to pray:
and when the evening was come, he was there alone.

But the ship was now in the midst of the sea,
tossed with waves: for the wind was contrary.

And in the fourth watch of the night Jesus
went unto them, walking on the sea.

And when the disciples saw him walking on the sea,
they were troubled, saying, It is a spirit;
and they cried out for fear.

But straightway Jesus spake unto them, saying,
Be of good cheer; it is I; be not afraid.

Gospel of St Matthew 14:23–27

July 25

And he brought him to Jerusalem,
and set him on a pinnacle of the temple,
and said unto him, If thou be the Son of
God, cast thyself down from hence:

For it is written, He shall give his angels
charge over thee, to keep thee:

And in their hands they shall bear thee
up, lest at any time thou dash
thy foot against a stone.

And Jesus answering said unto him,
It is said, Thou shalt not tempt
the Lord thy God.

Gospel of St Luke 4:9–12

July 26

And as Moses lifted up the serpent
in the wilderness, even so must the
Son of man be lifted up:

That whosoever believeth in him should not
perish, but have eternal life.

For God so loved the world,
that he gave his only begotten Son,
that whosoever believeth in him should not
perish, but have everlasting life.

Gospel of St John 3:14–16

July 27

Whatever is born of truth does not die.

Dialogue of the Savior
(trans. Emmel)

July 28

Then took Mary a pound of ointment of spikenard,
very costly, and anointed the feet of Jesus,
and wiped his feet with her hair: and the house was filled with
the odour of the ointment.

Then saith one of his disciples, Judas Iscariot,
Simon's son, which should betray him,

Why was not this ointment sold for three hundred pence,
and given to the poor?

This he said, not that he cared for the poor;
but because he was a thief, and had the bag,
and bare what was put therein.

Then said Jesus, Let her alone:
against the day of my burying hath she kept this.

For the poor always ye have with you;
but me ye have not always.

Gospel of St John 12:3–8

July 29

Whoever finds the world and becomes rich, let him renounce the world.

Gospel of Thomas 110

July 30

Fear not, little flock;
for it is your Father's good pleasure to
give you the kingdom.

Gospel of St Luke 12:32

July 31

And at even, when the sun did set,
they brought unto him all
that were diseased, and them that
were possessed with devils.

And all the city was gathered
together at the door.

And he healed many that were sick of
divers diseases, and cast out many devils;
and suffered not the devils to speak,
because they knew him.

Gospel of St Mark 1:32–34

August

August 1

Blessed are they that mourn:
for they shall be comforted.

Gospel of St Matthew 5:4

August 2

And there came a leper to him, beseeching him, and kneeling down to him, and saying unto him, If thou wilt, thou canst make me clean.

And Jesus, moved with compassion, put forth his hand, and touched him, and saith unto him, I will; be thou clean.

And as soon as he had spoken, immediately the leprosy departed from him, and he was cleansed.

Gospel of St Mark 1:40–42

August 3

The Law of Universal Genesis was the firstborn nous;
the second Chaos shed by the firstborn.
The third was received by the soul [...]
Clad in the shape of a hind she is worn away with death's
slavery, Now she has mastery and glimpses light:
now she is plunged in misery and weeps.
Now she is mourned, and her self rejoices.
Now she weeps and is finally condemned.
Now she is condemned and finally dies.
And now she reaches the point where hemmed in by evil,
she knows no way out. Misled, she has entered a labyrinth.
Then Jesus said 'Behold, Father,
she wanders the earth pursued by evil.
Far from thy Breath she is going astray.
She is trying to flee bitter Chaos,
and does not know how she is to escape.
Send me forth, O Father, therefore, and I,
bearing the seal shall descend and wander all Aeons through,
all mysteries reveal. I shall manifest the forms
of the gods and teach them the secrets
of the holy way which I call Gnosis [...]'

Dialogue of the Saviour
(trans. Roberts–Donaldson)

August 4

Verily, verily, I say unto you,
The hour is coming, and now is, when
the dead shall hear the voice of the Son
of God: and they that hear shall live.

For as the Father hath life in himself;
so hath he given to the Son
to have life in himself;

Gospel of St John 5:25–26

August 5

And the devil, taking him up into an
high mountain, shewed unto him all
the kingdoms of the world in
a moment of time.

And the devil said unto him,
All this power will I give thee, and the
glory of them: for that is delivered unto
me; and to whomsoever I will I give it.

If thou therefore wilt worship me,
all shall be thine.

And Jesus answered and said unto him,
Get thee behind me, Satan: for it is
written, Thou shalt worship the Lord thy
God, and him only shalt thou serve.

Gospel of St Luke 4:5–8

August 6

For he that hath, to him shall be given:
and he that hath not, from him shall be
taken even that which he hath.

Gospel of St Mark 4:25

August 7

Now there stood by the cross of Jesus his mother, and his mother's sister, Mary the wife of Cleophas, and Mary Magdalene.

When Jesus therefore saw his mother, and the disciple standing by, whom he loved, he saith unto his mother, Woman, behold thy son!

Then saith he to the disciple, Behold thy mother! And from that hour that disciple took her unto his own home.

Gospel of St John 19:25–27

August 8

Two men went up into the temple to pray;
the one a Pharisee, and the other a publican.

The Pharisee stood and prayed thus with himself, God,
I thank thee, that I am not as other men are, extortioners,
unjust, adulterers, or even as this publican.

I fast twice in the week, I give tithes of all that I possess.

And the publican, standing afar off, would not lift up so much
as his eyes unto heaven, but smote upon his breast, saying,
God be merciful to me a sinner.

I tell you, this man went down to his house justified rather
than the other: for every one that exalteth himself shall be
abased; and he that humbleth himself shall be exalted.

Gospel of St Luke 18:10–14

August 9

Peter said to him, Since you have explained everything to us, tell us this also: What is the sin of the world?

The Saviour said There is no sin, but it is you who make sin when you do the things that are like the nature of adultery, which is called sin.

Gospel According to Mary Magdalene 4:25–26

August 10

For every one that doeth evil hateth the light, neither cometh to the light, lest his deeds should be reproved.

But he that doeth truth cometh to the light, that his deeds may be made manifest, that they are wrought in God.

Gospel of St John 3:20–21

August 11

Everyone who has known himself
has seen it (that place of life and light)
in everything given him to do.

Whoever does not know the work of
perfection knows nothing.

Dialogue of the Savior
(trans. Emmel)

August 12

A certain man went down from Jerusalem to Jericho, and fell
among thieves, which stripped him of his raiment, and
wounded him, and departed, leaving him half dead.

And by chance there came down a certain priest that way: and
when he saw him, he passed by on the other side.

And likewise a Levite, when he was at the place, came and
looked on him, and passed by on the other side.

But a certain Samaritan, as he journeyed, came where he was:
and when he saw him, he had compassion on him,

And went to him, and bound up his wounds, pouring in oil
and wine, and set him on his own beast, and brought him to
an inn, and took care of him.

Which now of these three, thinkest thou, was neighbour
unto him that fell among the thieves?

And he said, He that shewed mercy on him.
Then said Jesus unto him, Go, and do thou likewise.

Gospel of Saint Luke 10:30–34;36–37

August 13

Why do you wash the outside of the cup?
Do you not realize that
he who made the inside is the same
one who made the outside?

Gospel Of Thomas 89

August 14

And Jesus answering said unto them,
Render to Caesar the things
that are Caesar's,
and to God the things that are God's.

Gospel of St Mark 12:17

August 15

The soul answered and said,
'What binds me has been slain,
and what surrounds me has been
overcome, and my desire has been ended
and ignorance has died.'

Gospel According to Mary Magdalene 8:21–22

August 16

And I say unto you, Ask,
and it shall be given you; seek,
and ye shall find; knock,
and it shall be opened unto you.

For every one that asketh receiveth;
and he that seeketh findeth;
and to him that knocketh
it shall be opened.

Gospel of St Luke 11:9–10

August 17

Then came to him the disciples of John,
saying, Why do we and the Pharisees fast
oft, but thy disciples fast not?

And Jesus said unto them, Can the children
of the bridechamber mourn, as long as the
bridegroom is with them? but the days will
come, when the bridegroom shall be taken
from them, and then shall they fast.

Gospel of St John 9:14–15

August 18

And again he entered into Capernaum, after some days;
and it was noised that he was in the house.

And straightway many were gathered together, insomuch that
there was no room to receive them, no, not so much as about
the door: and he preached the word unto them.

And they come unto him, bringing one sick
of the palsy, which was borne of four.

And when they could not come nigh unto him
for the press, they uncovered the roof where he was:
and when they had broken it up, they let down the bed
wherein the sick of the palsy lay.

When Jesus saw their faith, he said unto the sick of the palsy,
Son, thy sins be forgiven thee.

Gospel of St Mark 2:3–5

August 19

Ye have heard that it was said
by them of old time, Thou shalt not kill;
and whosoever shall kill shall be in
danger of the judgment:

But I say unto you,
That whosoever is angry with
his brother without a cause shall be
in danger of the judgment:
and whosoever shall say to his brother,
Raca, shall be in danger of the council:
but whosoever shall say,
Thou fool, shall be in danger of hell fire.

Gospel of St Matthew 5:21–22

August 20

The man old in days will not hesitate to ask a small child seven days old about the place of life, and he will live. For many who are first will become last, and they will become one and the same.

Gospel Of Thomas 4

August 21

Jesus answered them and said,
Verily, verily, I say unto you,
Ye seek me, not because ye saw the
miracles, but because ye did eat of the
loaves, and were filled.

Gospel of St John 6:26

August 22

If you become my disciples
and listen to my words,
these stones will minister to you.
For there are five trees for you in Paradise
which remain undisturbed summer and
winter and whose leaves do not fall.
Whoever becomes acquainted with
them will not experience death.

Gospel Of Thomas 19

August 23

And he said, So is the kingdom of God,
as if a man should cast seed
into the ground;

And should sleep, and rise night and day,
and the seed should spring and grow up,
he knoweth not how.

For the earth bringeth forth fruit of
herself; first the blade, then the ear,
after that the full corn in the ear.

Gospel of St Mark 4:26–28

August 24

It is the one who speaks who also listens,
and it is the one who can see who
also reveals.

Dialogue of the Savior
(trans. Emmel)

August 25

That is why the Good came into your midst, to the essence of every nature in order to restore it to its root.

Gospel According to Mary Magdalene 4:27

August 26

I will arise and go to my father, and will say unto him,
Father, I have sinned against heaven, and before thee,

And am no more worthy to be called thy son:
make me as one of thy hired servants.

And he arose, and came to his father.
But when he was yet a great way off, his father saw him, and had
compassion, and ran, and fell on his neck, and kissed him.

And the son said unto him, Father, I have sinned against heaven,
and in thy sight, and am no more worthy to be called thy son.

But the father said to his servants, Bring forth the best robe, and
put it on him; and put a ring on his hand, and shoes on his feet:

And bring hither the fatted calf, and kill it;
and let us eat, and be merry:

For this my son was dead, and is alive again;
he was lost, and is found.

Gospel of St Luke 15:11–32

August 27

In a [world] I was released from a world,
[and] in a type from a heavenly type, and
(from) the fetter of oblivion which is
transient. From this time on will I attain to
the rest of the time, of the season, of the
aeon, in silence.

Gospel According to Mary Magdalene 8:23–24

August 28

And when he was come into
his own country, he taught them in their
synagogue, insomuch that they
were astonished, and said,
Whence hath this man this wisdom,
and these mighty works?

Is not this the carpenter's son?
is not his mother called Mary?
and his brethren, James, and Joses, and
Simon, and Judas?

And his sisters, are they not all with us?
Whence then hath this man
all these things?

Gospel of St Matthew 13:54–56

August 29

And he went forth again by the sea side; and all the multitude resorted unto him, and he taught them.

And as he passed by, he saw Levi the son of Alphaeus sitting at the receipt of custom, and said unto him, Follow me. And he arose and followed him.

And it came to pass, that, as Jesus sat at meat in his house, many publicans and sinners sat also together with Jesus and his disciples: for there were many, and they followed him.

Gospel of St Mark 2:13–15

August 30

He that is faithful in that which is least
is faithful also in much:
and he that is unjust in the least
is unjust also in much.

Gospel of St Luke 16:10

August 31

Love your brother like your soul,
guard him like the pupil of your eye.

Gospel Of Thomas 25

September

September 1

Labour not for the meat which perisheth,
but for that meat which endureth
unto everlasting life, which the
Son of man shall give unto you:
for him hath God the Father sealed.

Gospel of St John 6:27

September 2

And when they had sent away the multitude,
they took him even as he was in the ship.
And there were also with him other little ships.

And there arose a great storm of wind,
and the waves beat into the ship, so that it was now full.

And he was in the hinder part of the ship,
asleep on a pillow: and they awake him, and say unto him,
Master, carest thou not that we perish?

And he arose, and rebuked the wind, and said unto the sea,
Peace, be still. And the wind ceased,
and there was a great calm.

And he said unto them, Why are ye so fearful?
how is it that ye have no faith?

And they feared exceedingly, and said one to another,
What manner of man is this,
that even the wind and the sea obey him?

Gospel of St Mark 4:36–41

September 3

For I say unto you,
That except your righteousness
shall exceed the righteousness
of the scribes and Pharisees,
ye shall in no case enter into the
kingdom of heaven.

Gospel of St Matthew 5:20

September 4

The Lamp of the body is the mind.

Dialogue of the Savior
(trans. Emmel)

September 5

If any man have ears to hear,
let him hear.

Gospel of St Mark 4:9

September 6

If, therefore, all the words which were spoken by the prophets have been fulfilled in me (for I myself was in them), how much more shall that which I say unto you come to pass indeed, that he which sent me may be glorified by you and by them that believe on me?

Epistle of the Apostles 19

September 7

If a son shall ask bread of any of you
that is a father, will he give him a stone?
or if he ask a fish, will he for a fish
give him a serpent?

Or if he shall ask an egg, will he offer
him a scorpion?

Gospel of St Luke 11:11–12

September 8

I would keep tune with holy souls. In me
know thou the word of wisdom.

Gospel of St Mark 5:1–13

September 9

Sell that ye have, and give alms;
provide yourselves bags which wax not old,
a treasure in the heavens that faileth not,
where no thief approacheth, neither moth
corrupteth.

Gospel of St Luke 12:33

September 10

Whoever has something in his hand
will receive more, and whoever
has nothing will be deprived of even
the little he has.

Gospel Of Thomas 41

September 11

Ye have heard that it hath been said,
An eye for an eye,
and a tooth for a tooth:

But I say unto you,
That ye resist not evil: but
whosoever shall smite thee on thy right
cheek, turn to him the other also.

Gospel of St Matthew 5:38–39

September 12

The majesty and authority are in him
since he embraces the whole of the
totalities, while nothing embraces him.
For he is all mind. And he is thought and
considering and reflecting and
rationality and power.

Sophia of Jesus Christ

September 13

And he said, Whereunto shall we liken the kingdom of God? or with what comparison shall we compare it?

It is like a grain of mustard seed, which, when it is sown in the earth, is less than all the seeds that be in the earth:

But when it is sown, it groweth up, and becometh greater than all herbs, and shooteth out great branches; so that the fowls of the air may lodge under the shadow of it.

Gospel of St Mark 4:30–32

September 14

By the Truth I tell you,
as a sick person looks at food
and does not taste its pleasure
because of the severity of his pain,
the companions of the world are the same.
He neither receives pleasure by worship
and does not find its sweetness with what he finds
from the love of the world.
By the Truth I tell you, surely the ride if it is not
ridden and prepared becomes difficult and its manner changed.
Hearts are the same, if they are not softened by
the remembrance of death and the share of worshipping,
they become hard and tough.

al-Ghazali,
The Revival of the Religious Sciences

September 15

For whosoever will save his life
shall lose it; but whosoever shall lose his
life for my sake and the gospel's,
the same shall save it.

Gospel of St Mark 8:35

September 16

Thou, O lord, art my defender:
thou art my worship,
and the lifter of my head.

Epistle of the Apostles

September 17

My bread is hunger,
my banner fear,
my clothes are wool,
and my prayer in winter is at sun rise,
and my lamp is the moon.
My ride is my legs,
my food and fruit whatever
the earth produces.
I spend the night and have nothing,
I awake in the morning
and have nothing,
and there is no one upon earth
more richer than I

al-Ghazali,
The Revival of the Religious Sciences

September 18

Whosoever therefore shall break
one of these least commandments,
and shall teach men so, he shall be called
the least in the kingdom of heaven:
but whosoever shall do and teach them,
the same shall be called great in the
kingdom of heaven.

Gospel of St Matthew 5:19

September 19

And when it was evening, his disciples came to him, saying,
This is a desert place, and the time is now past;
send the multitude away, that they may go into the villages,
and buy themselves victuals.

But Jesus said unto them, They need not depart;
give ye them to eat.

And they say unto him, We have here but five loaves,
and two fishes.

He said, Bring them hither to me.

And he commanded the multitude to sit down on the grass,
and took the five loaves, and the two fishes,
and looking up to heaven, he blessed, and brake, and gave the
loaves to his disciples, and the disciples to the multitude.

And they did all eat, and were filled: and they took up of the
fragments that remained twelve baskets full.

And they that had eaten were about five thousand men,
beside women and children.

Gospel of St Matthew 14:15–21

September 20

What man of you, having an hundred sheep,
if he lose one of them, doth not leave the ninety and nine in
the wilderness, and go after that which is lost, until he find it?

And when he hath found it,
he layeth it on his shoulders, rejoicing.

And when he cometh home, he calleth together his friends
and neighbours, saying unto them, Rejoice with me;
for I have found my sheep which was lost.

I say unto you, that likewise joy shall be in heaven over one
sinner that repenteth, more than over ninety and nine just
persons, which need no repentance.

Gospel of St Luke 15:4–7

September 21

It is written:
Suffer not thine ear to receive
aught against thy brother:
but if thou seest aught, correct him,
rebuke him and convert him.

Epistle of the Apostles 49

September 22

And Jesus went with him; and much people
followed him, and thronged him.

And a certain woman, which had an issue of blood twelve years,

And had suffered many things of many physicians, and had spent
all that she had, and was nothing bettered, but rather grew worse,

When she had heard of Jesus, came in the press behind,
and touched his garment.

For she said, If I may touch but his clothes, I shall be whole.

And straightway the fountain of her blood was dried up;
and she felt in her body that she was healed of that plague.

Gospel of St Mark 5:25–29

September 23

And I say unto you, Ask,
and it shall be given you; seek,
and ye shall find; knock,
and it shall be opened unto you.

For every one that asketh receiveth;
and he that seeketh findeth; and to him
that knocketh it shall be opened.

Gospel of St Luke 11:9–10

September 24

Be of good courage and rest in me.
Verily I say unto you, your rest shall be
above in the place where there is neither
eating or drinking, nor care nor sorrow,
nor passing away of them that are
therein: for ye shall have no part in the
things of the earth, but ye shall
be received in the everlastingness
of my Father.

Epistle of the Apostles 19

September 25

He says 'my Father who is in secret'.
He says 'Go into thy inner chamber,
shut thy door behind thee (and)
pray to thy Father who is in secret.'
This is He who is within them all.
Yet He who is within them all is the
Fullness – beyond Him there is
nothing further within.
This is what is meant by
'He who is above them'.

Gospel of Philip 74c

September 26

Everything that came from the perishable will perish, since it came from the perishable. But whatever came from imperishableness does not perish but becomes imperishable. So, many men went astray because they had not known this difference and they died.

Sophia of Jesus Christ

September 27

Believe ye that everything that
I tell you shall come to pass...
Verily I say unto you,
that I have obtained the whole power
of my Father, that I may bring back
into the light them that dwell in
darkness, them that are in corruption
into incorruption, them that are
in death into life, and that I may loose
them that are in fetters.

Epistle of the Apostles 21

September 28

And he cometh to Bethsaida;
and they bring a blind man unto him,
and besought him to touch him.

And he took the blind man by the hand,
and led him out of the town;
and when he had spit on his eyes,
and put his hands upon him,
he asked him if he saw ought.

And he looked up, and said,
I see men as trees, walking.

After that he put his hands again upon
his eyes, and made him look up: and he
was restored, and saw every man clearly.

Gospel of St Mark 8:22–25

September 29

Jesus was asked by some people,
'Show us the way by which we may
enter paradise.'

He said, 'Do not speak at all.'

They said, 'We cannot do that.'

He said, 'Then only say what is good.'

al-Ghazali,
The Revival of the Religious Sciences 3.87

September 30

Jesus answered and said unto him,
Verily, verily, I say unto thee,
Except a man be born again, he cannot
see the kingdom of God.

Gospel of St John 3:5

October

October 1

For what shall it profit a man,
if he shall gain the whole world,
and lose his own soul?

Gospel of St Mark 8:36

October 2

And Jesus being full of the Holy Ghost returned from Jordan,
and was led by the Spirit into the wilderness,

Being forty days tempted of the devil.
And in those days he did eat nothing: and when they were
ended, he afterward hungered.

And the devil said unto him, If thou be the Son of God,
command this stone that it be made bread.

And Jesus answered him, saying, It is written,
That man shall not live by bread alone,
but by every word of God.

Gospel of St Luke 4:1–4

October 3

I am that bread of life.

Your fathers did eat manna in the
wilderness, and are dead.

This is the bread which cometh down from
heaven, that a man may eat thereof,
and not die.

Gospel of St John 6:48–50

October 4

And as they were eating, Jesus took bread,
and blessed it, and brake it, and gave
it to the disciples, and said,
Take, eat; this is my body.

And he took the cup, and gave thanks, and
gave it to them, saying, Drink ye all of it;

For this is my blood of the new testament,
which is shed for many for the
remission of sins.

But I say unto you, I will not drink
henceforth of this fruit of the vine,
until that day when I drink it new with you
in my Father's kingdom.

Gospel of St Matthew 26:26–29

October 5

Suffer it to be so now:
for thus it becometh us to fulfil
all righteousness.

Gospel of St Matthew 3:15

October 6

And when they saw him, they were
amazed: and his mother said unto him,
Son, why hast thou thus dealt with us?
behold, thy father and I have sought
thee sorrowing.

And he said unto them, How is it that ye
sought me? wist ye not that
I must be about my Father's business?

And they understood not the saying
which he spake unto them.

Gospel of St Luke 2:48–50

October 7

If ye then, being evil, know how to give
good gifts unto your children:
how much more shall your heavenly
Father give the Holy Spirit
to them that ask him?

Gospel of St Luke 11:13

October 8

I am the hope of them that despair,
the helper of them that have no saviour,
the wealth of the poor,
the health of the sick,
and the resurrection of the dead.

Epistle of the Apostles 21

October 9

I am good: mild and gracious and
merciful, strong and righteous, wonderful
and holy: I am good. Alleluia.
I am meek and gentle.
Alleluia. Glory to thee, O Lord.

Gospel of Bartholomew 4:70
in *The Apocryphal New Testament*
trans. MR James

October 10

Ye shall behold a light,
more excellent than which shineth
and is more perfect than perfection.
And the son shall become perfect
through the Father who is light,
for the Father is perfect which bringeth
about death and resurrection.

Epistle of the Apostles 19

October 11

If thou canst believe,
all things are possible to him
that believeth.

Gospel of St Mark 9:23

October 12

That which you have will save
you if you bring it forth from yourselves.
That which you do not have
within you will kill you if you do not
have it within you.

Gospel Of Thomas 70

October 13

Blessed are the meek:
for they shall inherit the earth.

Gospel of St Matthew 5:5

October 14

And Jesus looking upon them saith,
With men it is impossible,
but not with God:
for with God all things are possible.

Gospel of St Mark 10:27

October 15

So that servant came, and shewed his lord these things. Then
the master of the house being angry said to his servant, Go
out quickly into the streets and lanes of the city, and bring in
hither the poor, and the maimed, and the halt, and the blind.

And the servant said, Lord, it is done as thou hast
commanded, and yet there is room.

And the lord said unto the servant, Go out into the highways
and hedges, and compel them to come in,
that my house may be filled.

For I say unto you, That none of those men which were
bidden shall taste of my supper.

Gospel of St Luke 14:21–24

October 16

Verily I say unto you,
the resurrection of the flesh shall
come to pass with the soul therein
and the spirit.

Epistle of the Apostles 24

October 17

And, behold, there was a woman
which had a spirit of infirmity eighteen
years, and was bowed together,
and could in no wise lift up herself.

And when Jesus saw her,
he called her to him, and said unto her,
Woman, thou art loosed from thine
infirmity.

And he laid his hands on her:
and immediately she was made straight,
and glorified God.

Gospel of St Luke 13:11–13

October 18

For not all true things are to be
said to all men.

Secret Gospel According to Mark

October 19

And whosoever shall offend one
of these little ones that believe in me,
it is better for him that a
millstone were hanged about his neck,
and he were cast into the sea.

Gospel of St Mark 9:42

October 20

Since it is infinite, he is ever
incomprehensible. He is imperishable
and has no likeness to anything.
He is unchanging good.
He is faultless. He is eternal.
He is blessed. While he is not known,
he ever knows himself.
He is immeasurable. He is untraceable.
He is perfect, having no defect.
He is imperishably blessed.
He is called the
'Father of the Universe'.

Sophia of Jesus Christ

October 21

I am the living bread which came down
from heaven: if any man eat of this bread,
he shall live for ever: and the bread
that I will give is my flesh, which I will
give for the life of the world.

Gospel of St John 6:51

October 22

He is the invisible Spirit, of whom it is
not right to think of him as a god, or
something similar. For he is more than a
god, since there is nothing above him,
for no one lords it over him. For he does
not exist in something inferior to him,
since everything exists in him.

He is eternal, since he does
not need anything.
For he is total perfection.
He did not lack anything,
that he might be completed by it; rather
he is always completely perfect in light.

Apocryphon of John

October 23

Neither do men light a candle,
and put it under a bushel, but on a
candlestick; and it giveth light unto all
that are in the house.

Gospel of St Matthew 5:15

October 24

What ye will, tell it me,
and I myself will tell you without
grudging: only keep ye my
commandments and do that which
I bid you and turn not away your face
from any man, that I turn not
my face away from you,
but without shrinking and fear and
without respect of persons,
minister ye in the way that is direct
and narrow and strait.

Epistle of the Apostles 24

October 25

He greeted them all, saying,
Peace be with you. Receive my peace unto
yourselves. Beware that no one lead you
astray saying Lo here or lo there!
For the Son of Man is within you.
Follow after Him!
Those who seek Him will find Him.

Gospel According to Mary Magdalene 4:33–36

October 26

And it came to pass, as he went into the house of one of the chief
Pharisees to eat bread on the sabbath day, that they watched him.

And, behold, there was a certain man before him
which had the dropsy.

And Jesus answering spake unto the lawyers and Pharisees,
saying, Is it lawful to heal on the sabbath day?

And they held their peace. And he took him, and healed him,
and let him go;

And answered them, saying, Which of you shall have an ass
or an ox fallen into a pit, and will not straightway pull him
out on the sabbath day?

And they could not answer him again to these things.

Gospel of St Luke 14:1–6

October 27

Answer the fool with his folly.

Secret Gospel According to Mark

October 28

Lord, how does he who sees the vision see it, through the soul or through the spirit?'

The Saviour answered and said, 'He does not see through the soul nor through the spirit, but the mind which is between the two - that is what sees the vision...'

Gospel According to Mary Magdalene 5:10–11

October 29

He that is not with me is against me:
and he that gathereth not
with me scattereth.

Gospel of St Luke 11:23

October 30

The images are manifest to man,
but the light in them remains concealed
in the image of the light of the father.
He will become manifest,
but his image will remain concealed
by his light.

Gospel Of Thomas

October 31

Thou that dancest, perceive what I do, for thine is this passion of the manhood, which I am about to suffer. For thou couldest not at all have understood what thou sufferest if I had not been sent unto thee, as the word of the Father. Thou that sawest what I suffer sawest me as suffering, and seeing it thou didst not abide but wert wholly moved, moved to make wise.

Acts of John 96
in *The Apocryphal New Testament*
trans. MR James

November

November 1

For whosoever exalteth himself
shall be abased; and he that humbleth
himself shall be exalted.

Gospel of St Luke 14:11

November 2

Be ye upright and preach rightly and teach,
and be not abashed by any man
and fear not any man, and
especially the rich,
for they do not my
commandments, but boast
themselves in their riches.

Epistle of the Apostles 46

November 3

It is the spirit that quickeneth;
the flesh profiteth nothing:
the words that I speak unto you,
they are spirit, and they are life.

Gospel of St John 6:63

November 4

And they lifted up their voices, and said,
Jesus, Master, have mercy on us.

And when he saw them, he said unto them,
Go shew yourselves unto the priests. And it came to pass,
that, as they went, they were cleansed.

And one of them, when he saw that he was healed,
turned back, and with a loud voice glorified God,

And fell down on his face at his feet, giving him thanks:
and he was a Samaritan.

And Jesus answering said, Were there not ten cleansed?
but where are the nine?

There are not found that returned to give glory to God,
save this stranger.

And he said unto him, Arise, go thy way:
thy faith hath made thee whole.

Gospel of St Luke 17:13–19

November 5

Heaven and earth shall pass away:
but my words shall not pass away.

Gospel of St Mark 13:31

November 6

That which hath fallen shall rise again
and that which was lost shall be found,
and that which was weak shall recover,
that in these things that are so created
the glory of my Father may be revealed.

Epistle of the Apostles 25

November 7

For every one that doeth evil hateth the light, neither cometh to the light, lest his deeds should be reproved.

But he that doeth truth cometh to the light, that his deeds may be made manifest, that they are wrought in God.

Gospel of St John 3:20–21

November 8

The Monad is a monarchy
with nothing above it.
It is he who exists as God
and Father of everything,
the invisible One who is above
everything, who exists as incorruption,
which is in the pure light into
which no eye can look.

Apocryphon of John

November 9

And if any man will sue thee at the law,
and take away thy coat,
let him have thy cloak also.

And whosoever shall compel thee to go a
mile, go with him twain.

Gospel of St Matthew 5:40–41

November 10

Matthew said to him: Lord, no one can find the truth except through you. Therefore teach us the truth.

The Saviour said: He who is ineffable.
No principle knew him, no authority, no subjection,
nor any creature from the foundation of the world until now,
except he alone, and anyone to whom he wants to make
revelation through him who is from First Light.
From now on, I am the Great Saviour.
For he is immortal and eternal. Now he is eternal,
having no birth; for everyone who has birth will perish.
He is unbegotten, having no beginning;
for everyone who has a beginning has an end.
Since no one rules over him, he has no name;
for whoever has a name is the creation of another.

Sophia of Jesus Christ

November 11

And Jesus answered him,
The first of all the commandments is,
Hear, O Israel;
The Lord our God is one Lord.

Gospel of St Mark 12:29

November 12

Let him who has grown rich
be king, and let him who
possesses power renounce it.

Gospel Of Thomas 81

November 13

When the unclean spirit is gone out of a
man, he walketh through dry places,
seeking rest; and finding none,
he saith, I will return unto my house
whence I came out.

And when he cometh,
he findeth it swept and garnished.

Then goeth he, and taketh to him seven
other spirits more wicked than himself;
and they enter in, and dwell there:
and the last state of that man
is worse than the first.

Gospel of St Luke 11:24–26

November 14

My soul is exceeding sorrowful, even unto death:
tarry ye here, and watch with me.

And he went a little further, and fell on his face, and prayed,
saying, O my Father, if it be possible, let this cup pass from me:
nevertheless not as I will, but as thou wilt.

And he cometh unto the disciples, and findeth them asleep, and
saith unto Peter, What, could ye not watch with me one hour?

Watch and pray, that ye enter not into temptation:
the spirit indeed is willing, but the flesh is weak.

Gospel of St Matthew 26:38–41

November 15

And when ye stand praying,
forgive, if ye have ought against any:
that your Father also which is in heaven
may forgive you your trespasses.

Gospel of St Mark 11:25

November 16

Then said the chief priests
of the Jews to Pilate, Write not,
The King of the Jews; but that he said,
I am King of the Jews.

Pilate answered, What I have written
I have written.

Gospel of St John 19:21–22

November 17

My doctrine is not mine,
but his that sent me.

Gospel of St John 7:16

November 18

By the Truth I tell you,
surely if the water-skin does not have a
hole in it or is damaged,
it is about to be a place for honey.
Hearts are the same,
if the desire does not have a hole in it
and greed does not soil it,
and luxury does not make it hard,
soon it will be a jug of wisdom.

al-Ghazali,
The Revival of the Religious Sciences

November 19

As the Father knoweth me,
even so know I the Father:
and I lay down my life for the sheep.

And other sheep I have, which are not of
this fold: them also I must bring,
and they shall hear my voice;
and there shall be one fold,
and one shepherd.

Gospel of St John 10:15–16

November 20

Blessed are they that have
not seen and yet have believed,
for they shall be called the children of the
kingdom, and they shall be perfect
among the perfect, and I will unto them
life in the kingdom of my Father.

Epistle of the Apostles 29

November 21

Children, how hard is it for them
that trust in riches to enter into the
kingdom of God!

Gospel of St Mark 10:24

November 22

Why have you come out into the desert?
To see a reed shaken by the wind?
And to see a man clothed in fine garments
like your kings and your great men?
Upon them are the fine garments,
and they are unable to discern the truth.

Gospel Of Thomas 78

November 23

But Jesus said unto them,
A prophet is not without honour,
but in his own country,
and among his own kin,
and in his own house.

Gospel of St Mark 6:4

November 24

Take heed therefore that the light which
is in thee be not darkness.

If thy whole body therefore be full of
light, having no part dark,
the whole shall be full of light,
as when the bright shining of a candle
doth give thee light.

Gospel of St Luke 11:35–36

November 25

From him who has not
shall be taken away.

Secret Gospel According to Mark

November 26

A certain man had a fig tree planted in his
vineyard; and he came and sought fruit
thereon, and found none.

Then said he unto the dresser of his
vineyard, Behold, these three years I come
seeking fruit on this fig tree, and find none:
cut it down; why cumbereth it the ground?

And he answering said unto him,
Lord, let it alone this year also, till I shall
dig about it, and dung it:

And if it bear fruit, well: and if not, then
after that thou shalt cut it down.

Gospel of St Luke 13:6–9

November 27

Increase your doing of a thing that the
Fire does not consume.
Whereupon it was asked:
'What is that?'
Jesus replied: 'Favours.'

al-Ghazali,
The Revival of the Religious Sciences

November 28

And he said, Abba, Father,
all things are possible unto thee;
take away this cup from me:
nevertheless not what I will,
but what thou wilt.

Gospel of St Mark 14:36

November 29

If any man will do his will,
he shall know of the doctrine,
whether it be of God,
or whether I speak of myself.

Gospel of St John 7:17

November 30

He who is near me is near the fire,
and he who is far from me is far
from the kingdom.

Gospel Of Thomas 82

December

December 1

If ye do not forgive,
neither will your Father which is in
heaven forgive your trespasses.

Gospel of St Mark 11:26

December 2

Go ye and preach mercifulness
of my Father, and that which
he hath done through me will I myself
do through you, for I am in you,
and I will give you my peace,
and I will give you a power of my spirit,
that ye may prophesy to them
unto life eternal.

Epistle of the Apostles 30

December 3

John, John, why do you doubt, or why are you afraid?
You are not unfamiliar with this image, are you? – that is,
do not be timid! – I am the one who is with you always.
I am the Father, I am the Mother, I am the Son.
I am the undefiled and incorruptible one.
Now I have come to teach you what is and what was
and what will come to pass, that you may know the things
which are not revealed and those which are revealed,
and to teach you concerning the unwavering race
of the perfect Man. Now, therefore, lift up your face,
that you may receive the things that I
shall teach you today, and may tell them to your fellow spirits
who are from the unwavering race of the perfect Man.

Apocryphon of John

December 4

It is I who am the light
which is above them all.
It is I who am the all.
From me did the all come forth,
and unto me did the all extend.

Gospel Of Thomas 77

December 5

Take heed to yourselves: If thy brother
trespass against thee, rebuke him;
and if he repent, forgive him.

And if he trespass against thee seven
times in a day, and seven times in a day
turn again to thee, saying, I repent;
thou shalt forgive him.

Gospel of St Luke 17:3–4

December 6

Why marvel ye that I raise the dead, or
that I make the lame
To go, or that I cleanse the lepers
Or raise up the sick, or that I have
healed the palsied and the possessed,
or that I have parted a few
loaves and satisfied many, or that I
have walked on the sea or that I
have commanded the winds? If ye
Believe this and are convinced,
Then ye are great.

Coptic Gospel (fragment)

December 7

Then shall the King say unto them on his right hand, Come,
ye blessed of my Father, inherit the kingdom prepared for you
from the foundation of the world:

For I was an hungred, and ye gave me meat: I was thirsty, and
ye gave me drink: I was a stranger, and ye took me in:

Naked, and ye clothed me: I was sick, and ye visited me: I was
in prison, and ye came unto me.

Then shall the righteous answer him, saying, Lord, when saw
we thee an hungred, and fed thee? or thirsty, and gave thee
drink?

When saw we thee a stranger, and took thee in? or naked, and
clothed thee?

Or when saw we thee sick, or in prison, and came unto thee?

And the King shall answer and say unto them, Verily I say
unto you, Inasmuch as ye have done it unto one of the least of
these my brethren, ye have done it unto me.

Gospel of St Matthew 25:34–40

December 8

The Spirit of the Lord is upon me,
because he hath anointed me to preach
the gospel to the poor; he hath sent me
to heal the brokenhearted, to preach
deliverance to the captives, and
recovering of sight to the blind, to set at
liberty them that are bruised,

To preach the acceptable year
of the Lord.

Gospel of St Luke 4:18–19

December 9

Thy kingdom come.
Thy will be done in earth,
as it is in heaven.

Gospel of St Matthew 6:10

December 10

The stone which the builders rejected is
become the head of the corner.

Gospel of St Mark 12:10

December 11

Let the fool walk in darkness.

Secret Gospel According to Mark

December 12

He was in the world,
and the world was made by him,
and the world knew him not.

He came unto his own,
and his own received him not.

But as many as received him,
to them gave he power to become the
sons of God, even to them that believe
on his name:

Which were born, not of blood,
nor of the will of the flesh,
nor of the will of man, but of God.

Gospel of St John 1:10–13

December 13

After this, Jesus knowing that all things
were now accomplished,
that the scripture might be fulfilled,
saith, I thirst.

Now there was set a vessel full of vinegar:
and they filled a spunge with vinegar,
and put it upon hyssop,
and put it to his mouth.

When Jesus therefore had received
the vinegar, he said, It is finished:
and he bowed his head,
and gave up the ghost.

Gospel of St John 19:28–30

December 14

For whosoever shall give you
a cup of water to drink in my name,
because ye belong to Christ, verily I say
unto you, he shall not lose his reward.

Gospel of St Mark 9:41

December 15

The example of whosoever
demands the world
is like those who drink sea water.
The more he drinks the more
his thirst increases
until it kills him.

al-Ghazali,
The Revival of the Religious Sciences

December 16

And if Satan rise up against himself,
and be divided, he cannot stand,
but hath an end.

Gospel of St Mark 3:26

December 17

Whosoever shall receive one of such
children in my name, receiveth me:
and whosoever shall receive me,
receiveth not me, but him that sent me.

Gospel of St Mark 9:37

December 18

Blessed are ye, when men shall revile you,
and persecute you, and shall say all manner
of evil against you falsely, for my sake.
Rejoice, and be exceeding glad: for great is
your reward in heaven: for so persecuted
they the prophets which were before you.

Gospel of St Matthew 5:11–12

December 19

How am I to speak with you about him?
His aeon is indestructible, at rest and
existing in silence, reposing (and) being
prior to everything. For he is the head of
all the aeons, and it is he who gives them
strength in his goodness.

Apocryphon of John

December 20

Verily I say unto you,
All sins shall be forgiven unto the sons
of men, and blasphemies wherewith
soever they shall blaspheme:

But he that shall blaspheme against
the Holy Ghost hath never forgiveness,
but is in danger of eternal damnation:

Gospel of St Mark 3:28–29

December 21

And this know,
that if the goodman of the house
had known what hour the thief
would come, he would have watched,
and not have suffered his house
to be broken through.

Be ye therefore ready also:
for the Son of man cometh at
an hour when ye think not.

Gospel of St Luke 12:39–40

December 22

For the law was given by Moses, but
grace and truth came by Jesus Christ.

Gospel of St John 1:17

December 23

And when Jesus was entered into Capernaum, there came
unto him a centurion, beseeching him,

And saying, Lord, my servant lieth at home
sick of the palsy, grievously tormented.

And Jesus saith unto him, I will come and heal him.

The centurion answered and said, Lord,
I am not worthy that thou shouldest come under my roof:
but speak the word only, and my servant shall be healed.

For I am a man under authority, having soldiers under me:
and I say to this man, Go, and he goeth;
and to another, Come, and he cometh;
and to my servant, Do this, and he doeth it.

When Jesus heard it, he marvelled,
and said to them that followed,
Verily I say unto you, I have not found so great faith,
no, not in Israel.

Gospel of St Matthew 8:5–10

December 24

And thou shalt love the Lord thy God with all thy heart, and with all thy soul, and with all thy mind, and with all thy strength: this is the first commandment.

And the second is like, namely this, Thou shalt love thy neighbour as thyself. There is none other commandment greater than these.

Gospel of St Mark 12:30–31

December 25

And there were in the same country shepherds abiding in the field, keeping watch over their flock by night.

And, lo, the angel of the Lord came upon them, and the glory of the Lord shone round about them: and they were sore afraid.

And the angel said unto them, Fear not: for, behold, I bring you good tidings of great joy, which shall be to all people.

For unto you is born this day in the city of David a Saviour, which is Christ the Lord.

Gospel of St Luke 2:8–11

December 26

The kingdom of the father is like a
merchant who had a consignment of
merchandise and who discovered a pearl.
That merchant was shrewd.
He sold the merchandise and bought
the pearl alone for himself.
You too, seek his unfailing and enduring
treasure where no moth comes near to
devour and no worm destroys.

Gospel of Thomas 76

December 27

And he entered again into the synagogue; and there was a man there which had a withered hand.

And they watched him, whether he would heal him on the sabbath day; that they might accuse him.

And he saith unto the man which had the withered hand, Stand forth.

And he saith unto them, Is it lawful to do good on the sabbath days, or to do evil? to save life, or to kill? But they held their peace.

And when he had looked round about on them with anger, being grieved for the hardness of their hearts, he saith unto the man, Stretch forth thine hand. And he stretched it out: and his hand was restored whole as the other.

Gospel of St Mark 3:1–5

December 28

And the Word was made flesh,
and dwelt among us,
(and we beheld his glory, the glory
as of the only begotten of the Father,)
full of grace and truth.

Gospel of St John 1:14

December 29

Whoever finds himself is
superior to the world.

Gospel of Thomas 111

December 30

I and my Father are one.

Gospel of St John 10:30

December 31

A lamp am I to thee that beholdest me.
Amen.

A mirror am I to thee that perceivest me.
Amen.

A door am I to thee that knockest at me.
Amen.

A way am I to thee a wayfarer.

Acts of John 95
in *The Apocryphal New Testament*
trans. MR James

Sources

Brown, Paterson (trans.),
Gospel of Philip,
www.earlychristianwritings.com

Coptic Bible

Emmel, Stephen, *Nag Hammadi Codex
III (The Coptic Gnostic Library): The
Dialogue of the Savior v.5 (Nag
Hammadi Studies),* Brill, 1984

Epiphanius, St, *The Panarion:
Sects 1–46 (Nag Hammadi Studies),* ed.
Frank Williams, Brill, 1987.

Epistle of the Apostles,
http://wesley.nnu.edu/biblical_studies/n
oncanon/writing/episaps.htm

Essene Book of Jesus, The,
http://people.tribe.net/

al-Ghazali,
The Revival of the Religious Sciences,
Islamic Texts Society

*Gospel According to Mary Magdalene,
The,* Gnostic Society Library,
www.gnosis.org

Gospel of Pseudo-Matthew, The, Gnostic
Society Library, www.gnosis.org

Guillaumont, Antoine et al.,
The Gospel According to Thomas,
Brill, 1976

Holy Bible, The, King James Version

James, MR, *The Apocryphal New
Testament,* Clarendon Press, 1924

Lambdin, Thomas O (trans.),
The Gospel of Thomas,
Gnostic Society Library,
www.gnosis.org

Mack, Burton L., *The Lost Gospel: The
Book of Q and Christian Origins,*
HarperCollins, 1993

Macrae, George W. and Wilson, R.
McL., *The Gospel of Mary Magdalene,*
www.thenazareneway.com

Meyer, Marvin W.,
*The Secret Teachings of Jesus: Four Gnostic
Gospels,* Random House, 1984

Meyer, Marvin W., *The Unknown
Sayings of Jesus,* Harper San Francisco,
1998

Parrott, Douglas M., *Sophia of Jesus
Christ,* Gnostic Society Library,
www.gnosis.org

Riddle, M.B.,
The Clementine Homilies,
www.compassionatespirit.com

Roberts–Donaldson (trans.),
The Dialogue of the Saviour
(Excerpt quoted by Hippolytus in his
Refutations and attributed to the
Naasene Gnostics)

Robinson, James, ed.,
The Nag Hammadi Library in English,
HarperCollins, 1990

Smith, Morton, *The Secret Gospel:
The Discovery and Interpretation of the
Secret Gospel According to Mark,*
Dawn Horse Press, 2005

Szekely, Edmond, *The Gospel of the
Essenes,* C.W. Daniel, 1976

Williams, Francis E.,
The Apocryphon of James,
Gnostic Society Library,
www.gnosis.org

Wisse, Frederick, *Apocryphon of John,*
Gnostic Society Library,
www.gnosis.org